Introduction

This course of self study aims to help you understand and speak simple German, the sort of German you will need on a visit to Germany or a German-speaking country such as Austria or parts of Switzerland. It cannot promise that at the end you will be speaking German perfectly, but by enabling you to learn the most important words and expressions you will need to use on your trip, it will undoubtedly help to improve your experience of visiting the country and to get more out of your time abroad.

The course does not require a great deal of study or concentration, but it does offer more than a phrase-book and you will find that if you are prepared to spend a certain amount of time, even an hour or two here and there, in going through each unit in turn and testing your knowledge carefully, you will begin to acquire a basic knowledge of the language. Then take the book with you on your trip abroad, so that you can practise the words and phrases you have learnt. Don't be afraid to make mistakes – it's always better to 'have a go' and is usually greatly appreciated by your hosts.

The course consists of 20 units, each dealing with a particular aspect of a visit to Germany. Within each unit are groups of words and phrases with English translations. Look at them carefully and read them aloud, referring where necessary to the Pronunciation section. The exercises which follow are of two types: those which require a test of memory to see if you have remembered how to ask a question or say a phrase which has occurred on the previous page, and those which ask you to make a small adaptation of a given phrase to suit your own purposes. For example, in Unit 9 on the subject of shopping, you will find the expression *Ich möchte einen Pullover* (I want a sweater). Turn the page and you are asked to state that you want to change some money, and also that you want to buy a suitcase. In this way you will learn to pass the first 'acid test' of learning a language, which is being able to adapt given language patterns to any situation you choose.

How to Speak German

Vowels

Vowels in German may be pronounced long or short and must be learnt carefully. Note the umlauts **ä**, **ö** and **ü**.

a	long like *a* in *park*	**Tag**	**Name**
	short like *a* in *pan*	**danke**	**Nacht**
ä	long like *a* in *late*	**spät**	**Verspätung**
	short like *e* in *let*	**Gepäck**	**Getränke**
e	long like *a* in *mate*	**gehen**	**Meter**
	short like *e* in *met*	**Wetter**	**etwas**
i	long like *ee* in *deep*	**Linie**	**Dia**
	short like *i* in *pin*	**mit**	**bitte**
o	long like *o* in *bone*	**wo**	**verboten**
	short like *o* in *pot*	**Osten**	**Koffer**
ö	as *er* in *mercy*	**möchte**	**zwölf**
u	long as *oo* in *fool*	**Super**	**suchen**
	short as *oo* in *took*	**Pfund**	**hundert**
ü	No English equivalent. Round your lips as for whistling and say *broom*	**Süden**	**Brücke**

Diphthongs

In addition to the simple vowels above, learn the following diphthongs:

au	as *ow* in *cow*	**Frau**	**Rathaus**
äu	as *oy* in *boy*	**Verkäuferin**	
ei	as *i* in *mine*	**einmal**	**frei**
eu	as *oy* in *boy*	**Auto-bahnkreuz**	**teuer**
ie	as *ee* in *see*	**wieviel?**	**abbiegen**

Consonants

Most German consonants are similar to English ones. There are, however, a number of important exceptions:

ch	either like English *sh* at beginning of word	**Chef**	**Champignon**
	or *h* is silent like *ch* in *character*	**Chaos**	**Chor**
	elsewhere pronounced like *ch* is *loch*	**nicht**	**acht**
d	like English *d* at beginning of word	**Damen**	**Dorf**
	like English *t* at end of word	**Fahrrad**	**Moped**
g	always hard (except in final position)	**Wagen**	**geradeaus**
j	like *y* in *yellow*	**ja**	**jeder**
q	always followed by *u* and pronounced as English *kv*	**Quittung**	
r	rolled more than in English and usually guttural	**rot**	**Rechnung**
s	before vowels as English *z*	**sehen**	**Sitz**
	at end of word as English *ss*	**das**	**Gleis**
	in combination **sch** as English *sh*	**Schmidt**	**Fisch**
	in combination **sp** as English *shp*	**spät**	**Spargel**
	in combination **st** (at beginning) like English *sht*	**Straße**	**Stau**
	(in middle) like English *st*	**Briefkasten**	
ss	is often written ß in German. It is pronounced as a voiceless *s*	**heißen**	**dreißig**
v	like *f* in *face*	**verboten**	**viel**
w	like *v* in *vest*	**Wagen**	**wieviel**
z	like *ts* in *outside*	**zehn**	**Zeitung**

The German language is strongly stressed, which means it is important when speaking the language to put emphasis on the correct syllable. The following guidelines may be useful:

1 The stress is laid on the stem, or principal part of each word, not on the ending:

ha-ben, *geh*-en, *fahr*-en, *komm*-en

2 In compound words (that is, words made up of two or more elements) the stress is usually on the first part:

Bot-schaft, *Doppel*-zimmer, *Speise*-karte.

3 Prefixes which can be separated from the main part of the verb take the principal stress:

aus-gehen, *ab*-fahren, *an*-kommen.

4 Take care with words beginning with **ge-**. Where the **ge-** is not part of the basic word stem, the stress is on the *second* syllable:

Ge-*bir*ge	Ge-*fahr*	Ge-*flügel*	Ge-*müse*
Ge-*päck*	Ge-*schäft*	Ge-*tränke*	Ge-*witter*
ge-*kocht*	ge-*öffnet*	ge-*schlossen*	ge-*stohlen*

Introduction to German Grammar

This section contains only a very basic outline of German grammar and is mainly concerned with examples of German usage which occur in this book. It is not intended as a comprehensive guide.

1 The/a + nouns

All German nouns are masculine, feminine or neuter, and the word for *the* and *a* must be learnt with each noun. Here is an example of each form with an appropriate noun:

Masculine	Feminine	Neuter
der Koffer	**die Adresse**	**das Kind**
(*the suitcase*)	(*the address*)	(*the child*)
ein Koffer	**eine Adresse**	**ein Kind**
(*a suitcase*)	(*an address*)	(*a child*)

Notice that in German all nouns are written with a capital letter.

Each noun forms part of a group or declension and the form of the noun (and adjective) changes according to its particular function within the sentence (subject of the verb, object of the verb, etc.). It also changes in the plural. The following table contains examples of three nouns from regular declensions:

	Singular	*Plural*
Masculine		
Subject	**der** Koffer	**die** Koffer
Direct Object	**den** Koffer	**die** Koffer
Possessive	**des** Koffers	**der** Koffer
Indirect Obj.	**dem** Koffer	**den** Koffern
Feminine		
Subject	**die** Adresse	**die** Adressen
Direct Object	**die** Adresse	**die** Adressen
Possessive	**der** Adresse	**der** Adressen
Indirect Obj.	**der** Adresse	**den** Adressen
Neuter		
Subject	**das** Kind	**die** Kinder
Direct Object	**das** Kind	**die** Kinder
Possessive	**des** Kindes	**der** Kinder
Indirect Obj.	**dem** Kind	**den** Kindern

Here are some examples of different forms of *the* and *a* taken from the book:

Subject: **Die** Ampel ist rot. *The traffic light is red.*
Der Zug hat Verspätung. *The train is late.*

Object: Machen Sie bitte **den** Kofferraum auf. *Please open the boot.*
Einen Parkplatz suchen. *To look for a parking place.*

Possessive: Der Reisepaß **des** Mannes. *The man's passport.*
Die Handtasche **der** Frau. *The woman's handbag.*

Indirect Object: (used with prepositions such as **mit** (*with*), **auf** (*on*), **von** (*from, of*), **zu** (*to*), etc.)
Mit dem Auto fahren. *To drive.*
Auf der Autobahn ist ein Stau. *On the motorway there is a traffic-jam.*

2 Adjectives

In German the ending of the adjective depends on whether the noun it accompanies is masculine, feminine or neuter, and singular or plural. It also depends on whether it is preceded by the definite article (**der**, **die**, **das**), the indefinite article (**ein**, **eine**, **ein**), or it stands alone:

der grüne Apfel	die gute Reise	das deutsche Buch
ein grüner Apfel	eine gute Reise	ein deutsches Buch
grüner Apfel	gute Reise	deutsches Buch

The endings also vary according to the adjective's place in the sentence, and are thus too complex for most visitors' needs. It is in written German that they take on greater significance.

Adjectives usually come before the noun, but those that appear after do not change their endings:

Dieses Brot ist frisch. *This bread is fresh.*

Der Laden ist geschlossen. *The shop is closed.*

3 This and that

The word for *this* is **dieser** and the word for *that* is **jener**. These demonstrative adjectives follow the usual rules for agreement of adjectives:

Wieviel kostet dieses Zimmer? *How much does this room cost?*

Ich möchte jenen Pullover. *I would like that pullover.*

4 I, you, etc.

The full list of personal pronouns is as follows:

Singular		*Plural*	
ich	*I*	wir	*we*
du	*you (familiar)*	ihr	*you (familiar)*
er	*he*	sie	*they*
sie	*she*		
es	*it*	Sie	*you (formal)*

Note that there are two ways of saying *you* in German: **du** and **Sie**. **Du** is only used between family and close friends, and so for the purposes of this book **Sie** is the form to use. It is used in both the singular and plural with the third person plural form of each verb (see overleaf). In written German, unlike English, **Sie** (= *you*) always takes a capital letter whereas **ich** (*I*) does not, except at the beginning of a sentence.

5 My, your, etc.

Although the use of possessive adjectives in this book is limited to *my* and *your*, the full list is as follows:

Masculine/Neuter	Feminine	
mein	meine	*my, mine*
dein	deine	*your, yours (fam. sing)*
sein	seine	*his, its*
ihr	ihre	*her, hers*
Ihr	Ihre	*your, yours (form. s., pl.)*
unser	unsere	*our, ours*
euer	eure	*your, yours (fam. pl.)*
ihr	ihre	*their, theirs*

Note that for the purposes of this book, the form used for *your* is **Ihr, Ihre**:

Ist das **Ihr** Koffer? *Is this your suitcase?*

6 Verbs

In German, the form of the verb changes according to the subject (I, you, etc.) which dictates the ending in each case. Here are some tables giving examples of some common verb patterns. All these verbs are to be found in this book.

sein (*to be*)

ich bin	*I am*	wir sind	*we are*
du bist	*you are*	ihr seid	*you are*
er/sie/es ist	*he/she/it is*	sie sind	*they are*
Sie sind	*you are*	Sie sind	*you are*

Sind Sie Frau Müller?   *Are you Frau Müller?*
Ich bin Frau Jackson.   *I'm Mrs Jackson.*
Wie spät **ist es**?   *What's the time?*
Es ist zehn Uhr.   *It's ten o'clock.*

gehen (*to go*)

ich gehe	*I go*	wir gehen	*we go*
du gehst	*you go*	ihr geht	*you go*
er/sie/es geht	*he/she/it goes*	sie gehen	*they go*
Sie gehen	*you go*	Sie gehen	*you go*

Wie **geht's?** *How are you? (= How goes it?)*

haben (*to have*)

ich habe	*I have*	wir haben	*we have*
du hast	*you have*	ihr habt	*you have*
er/sie/es hat	*he/she/it has*	sie haben	*they have*
Sie haben	*you have*	Sie haben	*you have*

Der Zug **hat** Verspätung. *The train is late.*
Haben Sie etwas anzumelden? *Have you anything to declare?*
Ich habe Kopfschmerzen. *I have a headache.*

Other useful verbal expressions found in this book include:

ich möchte (*I would like*)
Ich möchte bezahlen. *I'd like to pay.*
Ich möchte ein Einzelzimmer. *I'd like a single room.*

das gefällt mir (*I like it*) (literally '*it pleases me*')
Der Pullover **gefällt mir**. *I like the pullover.*

ich kann (*I can* from **können** *to be able*)
Ich kann nicht schlafen. *I can't sleep.*

7 Asking questions and saying no

Asking questions is very simple in German. You just reverse the order of the subject pronoun and the verb. Thus:

Ich kann Ihnen helfen. *I can help you.*
Kann ich Ihnen helfen? *Can I help you?*

Was **trinken Sie**? *What are you drinking?*
Wo **wohnen Sie**? *Where do you live?*

Note also:
Wann **fährt der Zug ab**? *When does the train leave?*
Wer ist das? *Who's that?*

To say no, you simply insert the word **nicht**. Thus:
Ich verstehe. *I understand.*
Ich verstehe **nicht**. *I don't understand.*

Der Pullover gefällt mir. *I like the pullover.*
Der Pullover gefällt mir **nicht**. *I don't like the pullover.*

1   General Expressions

a. Yes, No   **b.** Hello, Goodbye   **c.** Please, Thank You   **d.** Mr, Mrs   **e.** The, This   **f.** I, My . . .

a. **ja**   *yes*
       nein   *no*

Sind Sie Frau Miller?	*Are you Mrs Miller?*
Ja.	*Yes.*
Ist das Ihr Koffer?	*Is that your suitcase?*
Nein.	*No.*

b. **Guten Tag!**   *Good morning/Good afternoon/Hallo!*

       Guten Morgen!   *Good morning!*
       Guten Abend!   *Good evening!*
       Gute Nacht!   *Goodnight!*
       Auf Wiedersehen!   *Goodbye!*
       Hallo!   *Hallo!*

Guten Tag, wie geht's?	*Hallo, how are you?*
Danke gut!	*Fine, thank you.*

c. **bitte/danke** — *please/thank you*
Entschuldigen Sie! — *excuse me*

Bitte schön!	*There you are. (when giving something to someone)*
Danke schön.	*Thank you very much.*
Es tut mir leid.	*I'm sorry.*

d. der **Herr** — *gentleman (Mr)*
die **Dame** — *lady*
die **Frau** — *woman (Mrs)*
das **Fräulein** — *young lady (Miss)*
der **Junge**, das **Mädchen** — *boy, girl*
das **Kind** — *child*

Wie heißen Sie?	*What's your name?*
Herr Miller.	*Mr Miller.*
Frau Jackson.	*Mrs Jackson.*

e. **der** (m), **die** (f), **das** (n) — *the*
dieser (m), **diese** (f), **dieses** (n) — *this*
ein (m, n), **eine** (f) — *a/an*
das ist — *that is*

Der Koffer.	*Suitcase.*
Die Handtasche.	*Handbag.*
Das Gepäck.	*Luggage.*

f. **ich** — *I*
du — *you (familiar)*
Sie — *you (formal)*
mein (m, n), **meine** (f) — *my*
dein (m, n), **deine** (f) — *your (familiar)*
Ihr (m, n), **Ihre** (f) — *your (formal)*

Ich bin Herr Miller.	*I'm Mr Miller.*
Meine Frau.	*(This is) My wife.*
Mein Mann.	*(This is) My husband.*
Ihr Koffer.	*Your suitcase.*
Ihre Handtasche.	*Your handbag.*

1 General Expressions

What are these called in German?

1   2

3 You meet Mrs Miller and wish her good morning. What do you say?

4 You arrive at the hotel during the day and greet the receptionist. What do you say?

5 The receptionist wants to know if you are Mrs Jackson. What does she say?

6 You are Mrs Jackson, so what do you reply?

7 The receptionist points to a suitcase and asks if it is yours. What does she say?

8 If it is not your suitcase how do you reply?

9 What does the receptionist say as she gives you your room key?

10 How do you thank her?

11 In the evening you meet your German acquaintance, Mr Schmidt. How do you greet him?

12 Ask him how he is.

13 What does he answer?

14 You want to introduce your wife to him. What do you say?

15 Say goodbye to Mr Schmidt.

- In German one says simply **Ja,** or **Nein,** rather than 'Ja, mein Herr' or 'Nein, meine Dame'.

- **Grüß Gott** is said instead of 'Guten Tag' in Southern Germany.

- **Gute Nacht** is said only before retiring for the night.

- Acquaintances always greet each other with a handshake. If you are invited to someone's house for a meal, it is much appreciated if you bring some flowers for the hostess (not red roses).

- **Bitte** has two meanings: it is used when asking someone for something and also when giving something to someone.

- **Fräulein** is only used to address girls and young ladies of up to approximately 21 years.

- **Here are some useful words:**

gut	*good*	**schwer**	*heavy*
schlecht	*bad*	**leicht**	*light*
groß	*big*	**heiß**	*hot*
klein	*small*	**kalt**	*cold*
billing	*cheap*	**alt**	*old*
teuer	*expensive*	**neu**	*new*
früh	*early*	**schnell**	*fast*
spät	*late*	**langsam**	*slow*
schwierig	*difficult*	**göffnet**	*open*
leicht	*easy*	**geschloßen**	*closed*
ein bißchen	*a little*	**sehr**	*very*
genug	*enough*	**mit**	*with*
zu	*too*	**ohne**	*without*

2 Arriving in Germany

a. Customs **b.** Documents **c.** Nationality

Anmeldefreie Waren
Nothing to declare

Anmeldepflichtige Waren
Goods to declare

a.

	der **Zoll**	*customs*
	verzollen	*pay duty on*
	das **Gepäck**	*luggage*
	der **Koffer**	*suitcase*
	die **Tasche**	*bag*
	der **Kofferraum**	*boot (of a car)*

Haben Sie etwas anzu-melden?	*Do you have anything to declare?*
Nein.	*No.*
Machen Sie bitte den Kofferraum auf.	*Would you open the boot, please.*

b.

	der **Ausweis**	*identity card*
	der **Reisepaß**	*passport*
	der **Führerschein**	*driving licence*
	der **Name**	*name*
	der **Vorname**	*first name*
	die **Adresse**	*address*
	die **Unterschrift**	*signature*
	unterschreiben	*to sign*

Paßkontrolle.	*Passport control.*
Ihren Ausweis, bitte.	*Your ID (passport), please.*
Unterschreiben Sie hier.	*Please sign here.*

c.

die	**Staatsangehörigkeit**	*nationality*
	Deutschland	*Germany*
die	**Bundesrepublik Deutsch-land**	*Federal Republic of Germany (West Germany)*
die	**Deutsche Demokratische Republik (DDR)**	*German Democratic Republic (East Germany)*
der	**Deutsche**	*German (man)*
die	**Deutsche**	*German (woman)*
	deutsch	*German*
	Österreich	*Austria*
die	**Schweiz**	*Switzerland*
	Groß Britannien	*Great Britain*
	England	*England*
der	**Engländer**	*Englishman*
die	**Engländerin**	*Englishwoman*
	englisch	*English, British*
	Kanada	*Canada*
der	**Kanadier**	*Canadian (man)*
die	**Kanadierin**	*Canadian (woman)*
	Australien	*Australia*
der	**Australier**	*Australian (man)*
die	**Australierin**	*Australian (woman)*
der	**Schotte**/die **Schottin**	*Scotsman/woman*
der	**Waliser**/die **Waliserin**	*Welshman/woman*
der	**Ausländer**	*foreigner (male)*
die	**Ausländerin**	*foreigner (female)*
die	**englische Botschaft**	*the British Embassy*
das	**britische Konsulat**	*the British Consulate*

Ich bin Engländer.	*I'm English.*
Ich verstehe nicht.	*I don't understand.*
Wie heißt das auf Deutsch?	*How do you say that in German?*
Sprechen Sie Deutsch?	*Do you speak German?*
Haben Sie eine englische Zeitung?	*Do you have an English newspaper?*

2 Arriving in Germany

What are these called in German?

1

2

3 The customs official asks you: **Haben Sie etwas anzumelden?** If you do not have anything to declare, how do you reply?

4 The customs official would like you to open your suitcase. What does he say?

5 What sign indicates the point where you must show your passport?

6 The border guard would like to see your passport. What does he say?

7 The border guard asks you: **Sind Sie Engländer?** If you are English, what do you reply?

8 If you do not understand, what do you say?

9 You would like to buy an English newspaper. How do you ask for one?

What are these three countries called in German?

10   11   12

– Visitors to West Germany who are resident in other member countries of the EEC need only carry an **identity card**. For other visitors a valid passport is normally all that is required. For further information contact the Consular Office of the West German Embassy.

– If you are **driving to West Germany** you need to take with you your vehicle log (registration) book, your driving licence and a current insurance certificate or International Green Card.

– The address of the British Embassy in Bonn is: Friedrich-Ebert-Allee 77, D-5300 Bonn 2. Here are the addresses of some other embassies:
United States: Deichmanns Ave, D-5300 Bonn 2.
Canada: Friedrich Wilhelm Strasse 18, D-5300 Bonn 2.
Australia: Godesberger Allee 107, D-5300 Bonn 2.
There are British Consulates in Stuttgart, Hamburg, Frankfurt, Hanover and Munich.

– German is spoken in the Federal Republic of Germany (FRG), the German Democratic Republic (GDR), Austria and parts of Switzerland.

– Tips for **car travel through the GDR to West Berlin:** Police checks are very strict and you are required to show your passport and driving documents. Traffic regulations should be closely adhered to. The speed limits are 100 km (62 mph) on main roads, 80 km (50 mph) on secondary roads and 50 km (32 mph) in towns and villages. Seatbelts must be worn and you are not permitted to leave the main transit highways.

– **Before travelling to the GDR,** contact your nearest embassy or consulate to obtain information on visa requirements, etc.

– The **border crossings** for cars between the Federal Republic and the German Democratic Republic are the autobahns at Lauenburg, Helmstedt, Herleshausen and Rudolphstein.

3 Driving a Car

a. Vehicles **b.** Roads **c.** Service Stations
d. Parking

a.

das **Auto**	*car*
der **PKW** (= Personen-kraftwagen)	*car*
der **LKW** (= Lastkraft-wagen)	*lorry*
der **Wohnwagen**	*caravan*
das **Motorrad**	*motorcycle*
das **Moped**	*moped*
das **Fahrrad**	*bicycle*

Mit dem Auto fahren.	*Drive the car.*
Der Autofahrer.	*Driver.*
Autovermietung.	*Car hire.*

b.

die **Autobahn**	*motorway*
die **Bundesstraße**	*major road*
die **Landstraße**	*secondary road*
der **Weg**	*path, way*
Umleitung	*Diversion*

	Ausfahrt	*Exit*
	Anlieger frei	*Local traffic only*
der	Stau	*traffic jam*
die	Raststätte	*rest stop*

Das Autobahnkreuz.	*Motorway intersection.*
Das Autobahndreieck.	*Motorway junction.*
'Auf der Autobahn 5 ist ein Stau von 10 km.'	*'On route 5 there is a 10 km traffic jam.'*
Die Straße nach Köln.	*The road to Cologne.*

c.

die	Tankstelle	*petrol station*
	tanken	*buy petrol*
das	Benzin	*petrol*
	Super	*4-star*
	Normal	*2-star*
	Diesel	*diesel*
	bleifreies Benzin	*lead free petrol*
das	Öl	*oil*
die	Reifen	*tyres*

Wieviel?	*How much?*
Voll, bitte!	*Fill it up, please.*
Dreißig Liter Super, bitte.	*Thirty litres of 4-star, please.*
Der Ölwechsel.	*Oil change.*
Bitte den Ölstand prüfen.	*Check the oil, please.*

d.

	parken	*park*
der	Parkplatz	*car park, parking*
das	Parkhaus	*multi-storey*
die	Garage	*garage*
die	Tiefgarage	*underground garage*
die	Parkuhr	*parking meter*
die	Parkscheibe	*parking disc*

Einen Parkplatz suchen.	*Look for a car park.*
Der gebührenpflichtige Parkplatz.	*Paying car park.*
Die Parkgebühren bezahlen.	*Pay the parking charge.*
Parken verboten!	*No parking.*

Breakdowns, Accidents → 20

3 Driving a Car

What are these called in German?

1 2 3

4 You would like to hire a car in Germany. What sign do you look for?

5 You are driving on the motorway and stop at a petrol station. The attendant wants to know how much petrol you need. What does he say?

6 You want the tank filled up. What do you say?

7 How do you ask him to check the oil?

8 You want 30 litres of 4-star petrol. What do you say?

Explain in German what the following traffic signs mean:

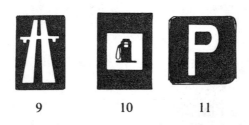

9 10 11

12 What does this mean?

13 You would like to leave the motorway. What sign do you look for?

14 What are these sections of the motorway called?

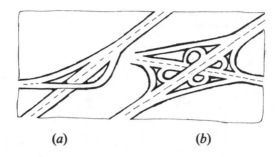

(a)   (b)

- **Speed limits** for cars are 100 km/h (62 mph) for major roads and 50 km/h (32 mph) in towns and villages. There are no speed limits on German motorways, although there is a recommended speed limit of 130 km/h. Take care not to hinder other cars, particularly if they are going faster than you are. Use your indicator to change lanes and always watch the traffic carefully in your rear-view mirror.

- The network of **motorways** extends over 4,600 miles and there are no tolls.

- Traffic rules are generally similar to those of other European countries. In fog, dipped headlights are compulsory. It is illegal to drive with sidelights only.

- There are three grades of **fuel**: *Super* (= 4-star petrol), *Normal* (= 2-star petrol) and *Diesel*. Prices vary and are often cheapest at independent petrol stations. They are usually slightly higher at motorway petrol stations.

- In some areas it is necessary to obtain a **parking disc** (*Parkscheibe*) which is a small plastic card with a clock dial which the driver sets and places inside the windscreen to indicate the time parked. These are obtainable at petrol stations, bookshops and tourist offices.

4 Finding Your Way

a. Maps b. In Town c. Streets d. Directions

<table>
<tr><td>a.</td><td>die Landkarte</td><td>map</td></tr>
<tr><td></td><td>die Straßenkarte</td><td>road map</td></tr>
<tr><td></td><td>der Stadtplan</td><td>street map, plan</td></tr>
</table>

Einen Stadtplan von München, bitte!	*A street map of Munich, please.*
Eine Straßenkarte von Norddeutschland, bitte!	*A road map of Northern Germany, please.*

<table>
<tr><td>b.</td><td>die Stadt</td><td>city, town</td></tr>
<tr><td></td><td>die Innenstadt</td><td>city centre</td></tr>
<tr><td></td><td>das Zentrum</td><td>centre</td></tr>
<tr><td></td><td>das Dorf</td><td>village</td></tr>
<tr><td></td><td>das Rathaus</td><td>town hall</td></tr>
</table>

Die Großstadt.	City.
Die Kleinstadt.	Town.
Wo geht es ins Zentrum?	How do I get to the city centre?

c.

die **Straße**	street
die **Allee**	avenue
der **Damm**	embankment
die **Gasse**	narrow street
der **Platz**	square
die **Brücke**	bridge
die **Ampel**	traffic light(s)
der **Zebrastreifen**	zebra crossing
der **Fußgänger**	pedestrian
die **Fußgängerzone**	pedestrian shopping precinct

Die Hauptstraße.	Main street.
Der Kurfürstendamm (in West-Berlin).	The Kurfürstendamm. (main street in West Berlin)
Die Einbahnstraße.	One-way street.
Die Ampel ist rot.	The lights are red.
Die Ampel ist grün.	The lights are green.
Wo wohnen Sie?	Where do you live?
Ich wohne in . . .	I live at . . .

d.

die **Richtung**	direction
Wo ist . . . ?	Where is . . . ?
abbiegen	turn
(nach) rechts	(to the) right
(nach) links	(to the) left
geradeaus	straight ahead
Norden, Süden	north, south
Osten, Westen	east, west

Wo ist das Rathaus?	Where is the town hall?
Geradeaus fahren.	Go straight ahead.
Nach rechts abbiegen.	Turn to the right.
Ist es weit?	Is it far?
Nein, es ist nicht weit.	No it's not far.

**Weights and Measures → 7, Places of Interest → 15,
Excursions → 16**

4 Finding Your Way

1 What do the following letters stand for in German?

2 You would like to buy a street map of Bonn. What do you say?

3 You would like a road map of Southern Germany. What do you say?

4 You arrive in a city and wish to drive to the centre. What sign do you look for?

5 You are in the centre of the city and are looking for the town hall. How do you ask a passer-by?

6 The passer-by tells you to drive straight ahead. What does he say?

7 The passer-by tells you to turn right. What does he say?

8 The passer-by tells you to turn left. What does he say?

9 You are driving on the autobahn and wish to go to Oberhausen. Which way do you go?

10 You are driving along a major road and want to go to Stuttgart. Which way do you go?

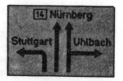

11 Say the names of these large cities in the 4 German-speaking states:
    Federal Republic of Germany: Kiel, Lübeck, Hamburg, Bremen, Hannover, Dortmund, Köln, Düsseldorf, Kassel, Frankfurt, Nürnberg, Saarbrücken, Mannheim, Stuttgart, München.
    German Democratic Republic: Rostock, Berlin, Potsdam, Magdeburg, Halle, Leipzig, Dresden.
    Austria: Innsbruck, Salzburg, Graz, Linz, Wien.
    Switzerland: Basel, Zürich, Bern, Genf, Luzern.

- Maps, town plans, information about places of interest and help with accommodation etc. can be obtained from the local **tourist offices** (Verkehrsamt, Verkehrsverein, Kurverwaltung, etc.) which are normally situated near the railway station or town hall.
- **Road signs**: West Germany follows the system of road signs that is used internationally, but here are a few common signs specific to German-speaking countries:

   Umleitung >

= One-Way Street   = Diversion

Bauarbeiten *Road Works*   Langsam *Slow Down*

Keine Einfahrt   *No Entry*

Durchfahrt Verboten   *No Thoroughfare*

- **Traffic signs** on the autobahn are white on a blue background. On major roads and country roads they are black on a yellow background.
- It is advisable to purchase up-to-date **road maps** and study them before your visit. Good maps can be obtained from the ADAC (Allgemeiner Deutscher Automobil-Club), tourist offices and book shops.
- Roads of particular interest to tourists are noted on the maps: **Bergstraße** (through the wine-growing region north of Heidelberg), **Deutsche Weinstraße** (through the wine-growing region of the Rhineland-Palatinate), **Romantische Straße** ('Romantic Road' in Bavaria), **Schwarzwald-Hochstraße** (in the Black Forest), etc.

5   Public Transport

a. Railways   **b.** Aeroplanes   **c.** Ships
d. Urban Transport   **e.** Information

a.

die	**Eisenbahn**	*railway*
die	**Deutsche Bundesbahn (DB)**	*German federal railways*
der	**D-Zug**	*express train*
der	**Intercity-Zug (IC)**	*express train stopping only at main cities*
der	**Eilzug**	*express train stopping at most stations*
der	**Nahverkehrszug**	*local commuter train*
der	**Wagen**	*carriage, coach*
der	**Bahnhof**	*railway station*
das	**Gleis**	*track, platform*

München Hauptbahnhof.	*Munich main station.*
Liegewagen.	*Couchette.*
Schlafwagen.	*Sleeping car.*
Der Kurswagen nach Stuttgart.	*Through coach to Stuttgart.*
Gleis 2.	*Platform 2.*

b.

der	**Flughafen**	*airport*
der	**Flug**	*flight*
der	**Flugschein**	*aeroplane ticket*
die	**Bordkarte**	*boarding card*
der	**Ausgang**	*exit, gate*
der	**Reihe**	*row*
der	**Sitz**	*seat*

Der Frankfurter Flughafen.	*Frankfurt airport.*
Den Flug nach New York buchen.	*Book the flight to New York.*
Bitte gehen Sie zum Ausgang 5!	*Please go to departure gate no. 5.*
Bitte anschnallen!	*Fasten your seatbelts, please.*
Die Sicherheitskontrolle.	*Security check.*

c.

der	**Hafen**	*harbour, port*
die	**Anlegestelle**	*docking area*
das	**Schiff**	*ship*

die	**Fähre**	*ferry*
das	**Deck**	*deck*
die	**Kabine**	*cabin*
die	**Überfahrt**	*crossing*

Der Hamburger Hafen.	*Hamburg harbour.*
An Bord gehen.	*Go aboard.*

d.

die	**U-Bahn** (= **Untergrundbahn**)	*underground*
die	**S-Bahn** (= **Schnellbahn**)	*suburban railway*
der	**Autobus**	*bus*
das	**Taxi**	*taxi, cab*
der	**Reisebus**	*long-distance coach*

Die U-Bahn-Station.	*Underground station.*
Die Bushaltestelle.	*Bus stop.*
Die Linie 12.	*Line no. 12.*
Hallo Taxi!	*Taxi!*
Zum Hauptbahnhof, bitte!	*To the main station, please.*
Zum Flughafen, bitte!	*To the airport, please.*

e.

die	**Information**	*information (desk)*
	Auskunft	*Information*
der	**Fahrplan**	*timetable*
	Ankunft	*arrival(s)*
	Abfahrt	*departure(s)*
die	**Fahrkarte**	*ticket*
die	**Rückfahrkarte**	*return ticket*
der	**Fahrpreis**	*fare*
der	**Zuschlag**	*surcharge (for certain trains)*
die	**Platzreservierung**	*seat reservation*
das	**Schließfach**	*luggage locker*

Einmal München, bitte.	*A ticket to Munich, please.*
Einmal Hamburg und zurück.	*A return ticket to Hamburg.*
Einsteigen bitte!	*All aboard!*
In Hannover umsteigen.	*Change trains in Hanover.*
Der Zug hat Verspätung.	*The train is late.*

Customs → 2, Times → 8, Money → 9

5   Public Transport

What do these signs stand for?

1

2

3   How do you call a taxi?
4   You want to go to the airport. What do you tell the driver?
5   You want to go to the main station. What do you say?

What sign do you look for at the railway station
6   if you want information?
7   if you want to check the train timetable?
8   if you want to buy a ticket?

Look at this ticket.

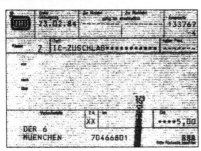

9   What does the abbreviation IC stand for?
10   What is a return ticket called?
11   You would like a ticket to Munich. What do you say to the clerk at the ticket window?

12   You are at the airport and have shown your ticket. The stewardess tells you to go to gate 5. What does she say?

- **Train fares** are about DM 18.–per 100 km (60 mi.). Ask for information on reduced youth, pensioners' and group fares, etc.

- A supplementary charge **(Zuschlag)** has to be paid on Intercity and certain express trains. Ask about this when buying your ticket. Intercity trains **(IC-Züge)** are fast, modern and comfortable. They have first and second class coaches and travel between the large German cities at hourly intervals. **TEE** (Trans-Europ-Express) trains are first class only.

- **Railway stations** in West Germany are open – there is no ticket control at the entrance to the platforms, but travellers are advised to buy their ticket before boarding the train. There are **automatic machines** for tickets for short journeys (up to 50 km).

- Foreign visitors who want to travel extensively on German Railways can obtain a **DB Tourist Card,** which is a special ticket offering unlimited travel within set periods, and without having to pay any supplements normally payable on the Intercity and fast trains. These tickets are also available to children aged 4 to 11 at half price.

- When boarding a train, make sure you get into a carriage travelling to your destination (this is indicated on the outside), as certain carriages are detached for rerouting on the way.

- **Frankfurt Airport** is the largest airport in Germany and one of the biggest in the world. One can get there by car, bus or S-Bahn. As the airport is a vast complex, it is advisable to obtain a plan to help you find your way around.

- The following German cities have an underground system **(U-Bahn):** Berlin, Hamburg, Hanover, Essen, Cologne, Dortmund, Frankfurt, Stuttgart, Munich, Nuremberg. Fares vary from city to city.

- All taxis have a taximeter. There is a basic charge of about DM3.–plus a rate per kilometre. If you want a taxi for a long journey, try and negotiate a fixed fare beforehand.

6 Accommodation

a. Hotels, Camping **b.** Hotel Rooms **c.** Prices
d. Toilets

a.

das	**Hotel**	*hotel*
die	**Pension**	*guest house*
das	**Privatzimmer**	*room rented in a private home*
der	**Campingplatz**	*campsite*
die	**Jugendherberge**	*youth hostel*

Ich suche ein Hotel.	*I'm looking for a hotel.*
Wo ist der Campingplatz?	*Where is the campsite?*
'Zimmer frei'.	*'Vacancies'.*

b.

die **Rezeption**	reception (desk)
das **Zimmer**	room
das **Einzelzimmer**	single room
das **Doppelzimmer**	double room
das **Bett**	bed
das **Bad**	bath
die **Dusche**	shower
der **Schlüssel**	key
die **Treppe**	stairs
der **Fahrstuhl**	lift
das **Stockwerk**	floor
das **Erdgeschoß**	ground floor, main floor

Ich möchte ein Einzel- zimmer für eine Nacht.	*I'd like a single room for one night.*
Ein Zimmer mit Bad.	*A room with bath.*
Ich habe ein Doppelzimmer reserviert.	*I have booked a double room.*
Es ist kein Zimmer frei.	*There are no rooms available.*

c.

der **Preis**	price
teuer	expensive
die **Rechnung**	bill

Wieviel kostet das Zimmer?	*How much is the room?*
Ich möchte bezahlen.	*I'd like to pay.*

d.

die **Toilette**	toilet
HERREN	Gentlemen
DAMEN	Ladies
besetzt	occupied
frei	vacant

Wo ist die Toilette?	*Where are the toilets?*
Dort hinten!	*Back there.*

Customs → 2, Parking → 3, Money → 9, Meals → 10

6 Accommodation

What are these called in German?

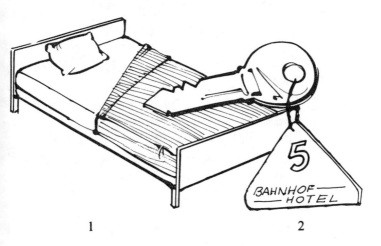

1 2

3 You are looking for a hotel and stop a passer-by to ask. What do you say?

4 Tell the receptionist you would like a single room.

5 Say you would like a double room.

6 The receptionist asks you: **Für wie lange?** (*For how long?*) How do you reply that you wish to stay for one night?

7 The receptionist says there is a room with a shower vacant. What does she say?

8 You really want a room with a bath. What do you say?

9 You want to know how much the room costs. How do you ask?

10 On the day of your departure you go to the desk to pay your bill. What do you say?

11 How do you ask where the toilets are?

12 You are looking for the campsite, and you stop a passer-by. What do you say?

13 You want to know where the youth hostel is. What do you say?

- There are three types of establishments offering **accommodation** in West Germany:
  Type R (Restaurationsbetrieb): hotel with restaurant.
  Type P (Pensionsbetrieb): boarding house offering meals to house guests.
  Type G (Garnibetrieb): bed and breakfast hotel offering breakfast only.
  Each type of establishment is graded I, II or III according to the facilities it offers, and rooms are also categorised 1, 2 or 3 (cat. 1 has bath/shower and WC).

- **Youth Hostels** (*Jugendherberge*) There are over 600 of these, open to members of any Youth Hostel association affiliated to the international YHA. A membership card can be obtained for a fee from the YHA in London or from the Deutsches Jugendherbergswerk Hauptverband, 26 Bülowstrasse, D-4930 Detmold, who will also supply a complete list of hostels on request.

- **Camping** There are over 2,100 campsites. Usually they are open from May to September. Charges vary and it is not normally possible to book in advance. Information can be obtained in Britain from the AA or RAC or the Camping Club of Great Britain. If you want a guide to the best sites in Germany, write to the German Camping Club, Mandlstrasse 28, D-8000 München 40.

7 Numbers, Weights and Measures

a. Numbers   **b.** Weights and Measures

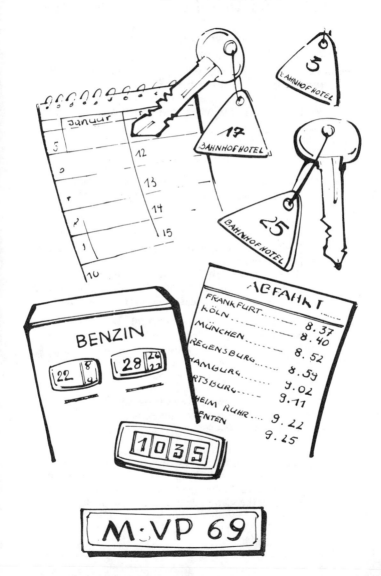

a.

0 **null**	10 **zehn**	20 **zwanzig**
1 **eins**	11 **elf**	21 **einundzwanzig**
2 **zwei**	12 **zwölf**	22 **zweiundzwanzig**
3 **drei**	13 **dreizehn**	30 **dreißig**
4 **vier**	14 **vierzehn**	40 **vierzig**
5 **fünf**	15 **fünfzehn**	50 **fünfzig**
6 **sechs**	16 **sechzehn**	60 **sechzig**
7 **sieben**	17 **siebzehn**	70 **siebzig**
8 **acht**	18 **achtzehn**	80 **achtzig**
9 **neun**	19 **neunzehn**	90 **neunzig**

100 **hundert**	800	**achthundert**
101 **hunderteins**	900	**neunhundert**
102 **hundertzwei**	1 000	**tausend**
120 **hundertzwanzig**	1 100	**tausendeinhundert**
200 **zweihundert**	2 000	**zweitausend**
300 **dreihundert**	5 000	**fünftausend**
400 **vierhundert**	10 000	**zehntausend**
500 **fünfhundert**	20 000	**zwanzigtausend**
600 **sechshundert**	100 000	**einhunderttausend**
700 **siebenhundert**	1 000 000	**eine Million**

b.

das **Gramm**	*gram*
das **Pfund**	*pound*
das **Kilo (kg)**	*kilogram*
der **Liter (l)**	*litre*
der **Meter (m)**	*metre*
der **Zentimeter (cm)**	*centimetre*
der **Kilometer (km)**	*kilometre*
Wieviel . . . ?	*How much . . . ?*
mehr	*more*
viel, eine Menge	*a lot*
wenig, ein wenig	*a little*

Ein halbes Pfund Butter.	*Half a pound of butter.*
Ein Pfund Kaffee.	*A pound of coffee.*
Ein halber Liter Milch.	*Half a litre of milk.*
Bis Köln sind es noch 100 km.	*It's another 100 km to Cologne.*

Times and Dates → 8

7 Numbers, Weights and Measures

Which rooms are the following guests staying in?

1 Mr Schmidt.

2 Mr Braun.

3 Mr Miller.

4 Mr Jackson.

5 Look at this Munich underground ticket. How much did it cost?

6 Read out the following distances in German:

(a)	Frankfurt–Köln	190 km
(b)	Frankfurt–München	400 km
(c)	Hamburg–Berlin	290 km
(d)	Hamburg–Hannover	150 km
(e)	München–Salzburg	130 km
(f)	München–Innsbruck	140 km

7   How much coffee is in this packet?

8   How much milk is in this carton?

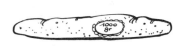

9   How many grams does this loaf of bread weigh?

10 How much does this piece of butter weigh?

- In Germany, **weights** are usually given in pounds (= 500 grams), i.e. 'halbes Pfund, viertel Pfund', etc. However the following conversion rates to the metric system should be noted:

1 kg = 2.2 lb	100 g = 3.5 oz
1 lb = 0.45 kg	250 g = 9.0 oz
1 l = 0.22 gal	1 km = 0.62 mile
1 gal = 4.54 l	1 mile = 1.6 km

- **Quantities** do not take the plural:

1 Mark	5 Mark	1 Liter	5 Liter
1 Pfund	5 Pfund	1 Meter	5 Meter
1 Kilo	5 Kilo	1 Kilometer	5 Kilometer

- Note the following peculiarities:
  sechs–sechzehn–sechzig
  sieben–siebzehn–siebzig
  dreißig–vierzig, fünfzig, . . .

8 Times and Dates

a. Telling the Time
b. Times of the Day
c. Week and Month

a.	die **Uhr**	clock, watch
	die **Stunde**	hour
	die **Minute**	minute
	der **Augenblick**	moment

Eine Stunde.	*One hour.*
Eine halbe Stunde.	*Half an hour.*
Eine Viertelstunde.	*Quarter of an hour.*
Wieviel Uhr ist es?	*What time is it?*
Es ist 10 Uhr.	*It is 10 o'clock.*
Halb 11.	*10:30. (= half to 11)*
Viertel nach, Viertel vor.	*Quarter past, quarter to.*
Wann/Um wieviel Uhr?	*When/At what time?*
Um 10 Uhr.	*At 10 o'clock.*
Von 8 bis 10 Uhr.	*From 8 to 10 o'clock.*

b.

der	**Tag**	*day*
der	**Morgen,** der **Vormittag**	*morning*
der	**Mittag**	*midday*
der	**Nachmittag**	*afternoon*
der	**Abend**	*evening*
die	**Nacht**	*night*
	Mitternacht	*midnight*
	heute/jeden Tag	*today/every day*
	morgen/gestern	*tomorrow/yesterday*

Wann reisen Sie ab?	*When are you leaving?*
Wann fährt der Zug ab?	*When does the train leave?*
Wann kommt er an?	*When does it arrive?*
Heute abend.	*This evening.*
Morgen früh.	*Tomorrow morning.*

c.

die	**Woche**	*week*
	Montag	*Monday*
	Dienstag	*Tuesday*
	Mittwoch	*Wednesday*
	Donnerstag	*Thursday*
	Freitag	*Friday*
	Samstag	*Saturday*
	Sonntag	*Sunday*
das	**Wochenende**	*weekend*
der	**Monat**	*month*
das	**Jahr**	*year*

Montags geschlossen.	*Closed on Mondays.*
Samstag, der 10 Juni.	*Saturday, June 10th.*
Nächste Woche.	*Next week.*

Public Transport → 5, Numbers → 7

8 Times and Dates

1 How do you express in German
   (a) a period of 60 minutes;
   (b) a period of 30 minutes;
   (c) the time of day from sunrise till noon;
   (d) the time of day from noon till sunset;
   (e) the period of darkness?

2 What are the following in German?
   (a) a period of 24 hours;
   (b) a period of 7 days.

3 You want to know the time. What do you say?

4 Say what time it is for each of the clocks below.

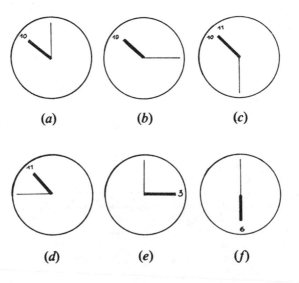

(a) (b) (c)

(d) (e) (f)

Look at this portion of the train timetable at Munich Main Station:

		Abfahrt der Züge in München Hbf	
Zeit	**Zug**	**in Richtung**	**Gleis**
8 34	E 3234 ⭢	Pfaffenhofen 9 04 – Wolnzach 9 12 – Ingolstadt 9 24 – Treuchtlingen 10 33 – Weißenburg 10 41 – Pleinfeld 10 48 – Georgensgmund 10 54 – Roth 11 00 – Schwabach 11 08 – **Nürnberg 11.21** Halt zwischen Ingolstadt und Treuchtlingen überall Verbund-Fahrausweise ungültig	20
8 38	E 3551 ⭢	Mu Ost ab 8 48 – Grafing Bf 9 05 – Rosenheim 9 23 – Raubling 9 32 – Brannenburg 9 37 – Flintsbach 9 40 – Oberaudorf 9 46 – Kiefersfelden 9 50 – **Kufstein 9.54**	4
8 43	🚅 518 **Patrizier** ◆ ✗	Augsburg 9 12 – Ulm 9 57 – Stuttgart 10 57 – Heidelberg 12.12 – Mannheim 12 27 – Mainz 13.11 – Koblenz 14 05 – Bonn 14 35 – Köln 14 57 – Dusseldorf 15.25 – Duisburg 15 39 – Essen 15 52 – Bochum 16 03 – Dortmund 16 18 – **Münster (Westf) 16.53** – Osnabruck 17 19 – Bremen 18 16 – Hamburg Hbf 19.14 – Hamburg Dammtor 19 20 – Hamburg-Altona 19 28	22

5 What time does the train for Nuremberg leave?

6 What time does it arrive in Nuremberg?

7 What time does the train for Hamburg leave?

8 What time does it arrive at Hamburg main station?

9 Someone asks you what time the train is arriving. Say it arrives at 7 pm.

10 You want to know what time the bus leaves. What do you say?

- The **months of the year** in German are: Januar, Februar, März, April, Mai, Juni, Juli, August, September, Oktober, November, Dezember.
- Note that one says '13 **Uhr**' (not '13 Uhren').
- Times after midday are expressed as follows:

In spoken German:	In written and spoken German:
1 Uhr (nachmittags)	13 Uhr
8 Uhr (abends)	20 Uhr

'20.30 Uhr' is expressed as 'zwanzig Uhr dreißig'.

9 Money and Shopping

a. Money **b.** At the Bank, Changing Money
c. Shopping **d.** Paying

a.	das **Geld**	*money*
	das **Kleingeld**	*change*
	der **Schein**	*(bank)note*
	die **Mark (DM)**	*mark*
	der **Pfennig**	*pfennig (100 pfennigs = 1 mark)*
b.	die **Bank**	*bank*
	die **Sparkasse**	*savings and loan association, bank*

die **Wechselstube**	*currency exchange*
der **Wechselkurs**	*exchange rate*
der **Reisescheck**	*traveller's cheque*
die **Kreditkarte**	*credit card*
die **Währung**	*currency*

| Wo ist eine Wechselstube? | *Where is there an exchange?* |
| Ich möchte 100 Pfund eintauschen. | *I'd like to change £100.* |

c.

	kaufen	*buy*
das	**Geschäft**	*shop, store*
das	**Kaufhaus**	*department store*
der	**Markt**	*market*
der	**Supermarkt**	*supermarket*
das	**Einkaufszentrum**	*shopping centre*
die	**Fußgängerzone**	*pedestrian precinct*
der	**Kunde**	*customer*
die	**Verkäuferin**	*shop assistant*
das	**Sonderangebot**	*sale item*

Kann ich Ihnen helfen?	*May I help you?*
Ich möchte mich nur umsehen.	*I'm only looking.*
Ich möchte einen Pullover.	*I'd like a pullover.*
Sonst noch etwas?	*Anything else?*
Danke, das ist alles.	*No thank you, that's all.*

d.

der	**Preis**	*price*
die	**Mehrwertsteuer (MwSt)**	*VAT*
	teuer	*expensive*
	billig	*cheap*
	bezahlen	*pay*
die	**Kasse**	*cash desk*
die	**Quittung**	*receipt*
der	**Kassenbon**	*cash register receipt*

Wieviel kostet es?	*How much does it cost?*
10 Mark. (DM 10,–)	*10 marks.*
Bar bezahlen.	*Pay in cash.*
Mit Scheck bezahlen.	*Pay by cheque.*

Numbers → 7, Clothing → 19

9   Money and Shopping

1   You want to exchange some money. What sign do you look for?

2   You would like to exchange £50. What do you say?

3   You enter a shop but do not wish to buy anything. What do you say to the shop assistant?

4   You would like to buy a suitcase. What do you say?

5   You would like to know how much it costs. What do you say?

6   When you have bought the suitcase, the assistant asks you if you would like anything else. What does he say?

7   You say *No, thank you.*

8   Say you want to pay by credit card.

9   What is a pedestrian shopping precinct called in German?

Here is a receipt from a department store.

10   What is the name of the store?

11   What city is it in?

12   What did the customer pay for the first item?

13   What did the second item cost?

14   How much did the customer pay altogether?

HERTIE
Berlin, Mehringdamm

1 3 OKT 85

00 01.38
00 03.98

7238 00 05.36 BAR

Kasse 109
Besten Dank · Auf Wiedersehen

- The **Deutsche Mark** is abbreviated to DM. The Mark is divided into 100 Pfennige (Pf). The Austrian unit of currency is the **Schilling**.

- **Shopping hours** vary but shops are generally open between 09.00 am and 6.30 pm. On Saturdays shops close at lunchtime except on the first Saturday of each month when they stay open till 6 pm. Many small shops close for lunch between 12.00 and 2 pm.

- **Banks** are open on weekdays from 8.30 am to 1 pm and from 2.30 pm to 4 pm. They stay open later on Thursdays (to 5.30 pm). Some important German banks are the Deutsche Bank, the Dresdner Bank and the Commerzbank. You can exchange money at any bank or exchange office—which at frontiers are open from 6 am to 10 pm every day.

- In Germany there are a number of large **department store chains** (Hertie, Karstadt, Horten, etc.) which offer a wide selection of goods at reasonable prices. The largest store in Germany is the KaDeWe in West Berlin. It is worth setting aside at least a morning or an afternoon to visit it.

- Here are the names of some of the most useful types of **shop**:
Bäckerei *baker*
Metzgerei *butcher*
Lebensmittel *groceries*
Fischmarkt/Fischgeschäft *fish market*
Konditorei/Bäckerei *patisserie*
Apotheke *chemist*
Buchhandlung *bookshop*
Eisenwarengeschäft *hardware-store*
Schuhgeschäft *shoe-shop*
Drogerie/Parfümerie *non-medical drugstore*

10 Meals

a. Meals **b.** Tableware **c.** Breakfast
d. Snacks

a.

das	**Frühstück**	*breakfast*
das	**Mittagessen**	*lunch*
das	**Abendessen**	*supper, dinner*
die	**Vollpension**	*full board*
die	**Halbpension**	*half board*
	essen	*eat*
	trinken	*drink*

Wir wollen frühstücken.	*We'd like breakfast.*
Ein Zimmer mit Halb-pension mieten.	*Rent a room with half board.*
Übernachtung mit Früh-stück.	*Bed and Breakfast.*

b.

die	**Tasse**	*cup*
das	**Glas**	*glass*
die	**Kanne**	*coffeepot/teapot*
die	**Flasche**	*bottle*
der	**Teller**	*plate*
der	**Löffel**	*spoon*
die	**Gabel**	*fork*
das	**Messer**	*knife*

Eine Flasche Wein.	*A bottle of wine.*
Die Kaffeekanne.	*Coffeepot.*
Eine Tasse Kaffee trinken.	*Drink a cup of coffee.*
Ein Glas Wasser.	*A glass of water.*
Zweimal Kaffee, bitte.	*Two coffees, please.*

c.

das	**Brot**	*bread*
das	**Brötchen**	*roll*
das	**Toastbrot**	*toast*
die	**Butter**	*butter*
die	**Konfitüre**	*jam*
das	**Ei**	*egg*
die	**Wurst**	*sausage*
der	**Käse**	*cheese*
der	**Kaffee**	*coffee*
der	**Tee**	*tea*
der	**Orangensaft**	*orange juice*
die	**Milch**	*milk*

Möchten Sie Kaffee oder Tee?	*Would you like coffee or tea?*
Eine Scheibe Brot mit Butter und Wurst.	*A slice of bread with butter and sausage.*
Ein Brötchen mit Butter und Konfitüre.	*A roll with butter and jam.*

d.

der	**Imbiß**	*quick bite, snack*
die	**Imbißstube**	*snack bar*
die	**Würstchen**	*pork sausages*
die	**Bockwurst**	*long red sausage, Frankfurter*
die	**Bratwurst**	*grilled sausage*
die	**Weißwurst**	*white sausage (Munich speciality)*
der	**Kartoffelsalat**	*potato salad*
die	**Pommes frites**	*chips*
der	**Leberkäse**	*spicy luncheon meat*

Eine Bockwurst mit Kartoffelsalat, bitte!	*A bockwurst with potato salad, please.*
Eine Bratwurst und ein Bier, bitte!	*A bratwurst and a beer, please.*

Paying → 9, Restaurants → 11, Drinking → 14

10 Meals

1 What are the three meals of the day called in German?

2 What are the following called in German?

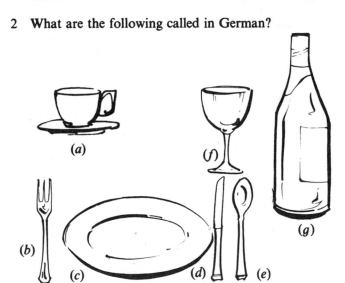

3 What are these called in German?

4 You are booking a hotel room. Say you would like a room with all meals.

5 How would you ask for a cup of tea?

6 You want a cup of coffee with milk. What do you ask for?

7 Say you would like a slice of toast with butter and jam.

8 You are in a snack bar. How do you ask for a grilled sausage with potato salad?

9 You would like a glass of wine. What do you say to the waiter?

10 How would you ask for sausages and chips?

- The **main meal** of the day in Germany is lunch. Breakfast and supper are not usually hot meals and in German homes consist largely of bread.
- **Mealtimes** in restaurants are as follows: breakfast until 10 am; lunch from 12.00 to 2 pm; and dinner from 6 o'clock till 9.30 pm.
- In Germany there are over 200 **types of bread** made from wheat and rye – white bread, mixed grain bread, rye bread, pumpernickel (black bread), etc. Brown bread is preferred to white bread, and it is sliced, not broken.
- German **Wurst** in its many varieties is world-famous. There are three main types: meat spread (e.g. Leberwurst, Mettwurst), fresh sausage meat (e.g. Jagdwurst, Zungenwurst), and smoked sausage meat (e.g. Cervelatwurst, Salami). Wurst is eaten on bread, and it is worth trying out the different sorts.
- **Cheese** is largely imported from Switzerland, Holland and France. Popular cheeses in Germany are Tilsiter, Edam and Emmentaler.

11 Restaurants

a. Restaurants   **b.** Service, Menu
c. Seasonings   **d.** The Bill

HIRSCH BRÄU
MÜNCHEN

a.

das **Restaurant**	*restaurant*
das **Café**	*café*
die **Weinstube**	*wine bar*
die **Theke**	*bar, counter*
der **Tisch**	*table*
der **Platz**	*seat*
der **Gast**	*guest*
die **Selbstbedienung**	*self-service*

Einen Tisch für vier (Personen) bitte.	*Do you have a table for 4?*
Entschuldigen Sie, ist dieser Platz noch frei?	*Excuse me, is this seat free?*
Nein, er ist besetzt.	*No, it's taken.*
Reserviert.	*Reserved.*

b.

die	**Speisekarte**	*menu*
das	**Tagesmenü**	*menu of the day*
die	**Weinkarte**	*wine-list*
das	**Gedeck**	*cover (charge)*
der	**Gang**	*course*
der	**Nachtisch**	*dessert*
	bestellen	*order*

Die Speisekarte, bitte.	*Bring me the menu please.*
Was ist das?	*What is this?*
Ich nehme Bratwurst und Kartoffelsalat.	*I'll have bratwurst and potato salad.*
Was trinken Sie?	*What would you like to drink?*
Einen Apfelsaft, bitte.	*An apple juice, please.*
Guten Appetit!	*Bon appétit!*

c.

der	**Zucker**	*sugar*
das	**Salz**	*salt*
der	**Pfeffer**	*pepper*
das	**Öl**	*oil*
der	**Essig**	*vinegar*
der	**Senf**	*mustard*

d.

der	**Ober**	*(head) waiter*
der	**Kellner**	*waiter*
die	**Rechnung**	*bill*
das	**Trinkgeld**	*tip, service*

Hallo! Herr Ober!	*Waiter!*
Hallo! Fräulein!	*Waitress!*
Die Rechnung, bitte.	*Bring me the bill, please.*
Ist das Trinkgeld inbegriffen?	*Is service included?*
Ich möchte zahlen!	*I'd like to pay.*
Zusammen?	*Together?*
Nein, jeder für sich.	*No, separate bills.*
Das macht 25 Mark.	*That'll be 25 marks.*
Stimmt so.	*That's fine./Keep the change.*

Toilets → 6, Paying → 9, Meals → 10, Drinking → 14

1   Where do you go
    (a) if you want lunch or dinner?
    (b) if you want coffee and cake?
    (c) if you want a glass of wine?

2   You are in a restaurant. Tell the waiter you want a
    table for 3.

3   You see an empty seat at a table and want to know if
    it is free. What do you say?

4   If the seat is taken, how does the person at the table
    reply?

5   Would you sit down at a table with the following
    card on it? (Answer **ja** or **nein**):

6   Tell the waiter you would like to see the menu.

7   When you have ordered your meal, the waiter asks
    you what you would like to drink. What does he say?

8   You would like an apple juice, so how do you reply?

9   You would like to pay. How do you ask the waiter
    for the bill?

10 The waiter wants to know if you are paying for
    everyone at the table. What does he say?

11 The bill comes to DM 60.–. You give the waiter DM
    65.–(DM 5.– as a tip). What do you tell the waiter?

12 What are the following seasonings called in German?

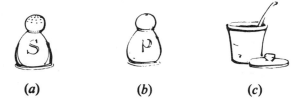

(a)   (b)   (c)

- In most restaurants and cafés, the guest seats himself and does not wait to be guided to a table. If the restaurant is full, it is quite acceptable to sit down at a partially occupied table after making sure that the seat is free.

- In a **café** you can order coffee and cake (or other small snacks). Before you sit down, choose your cake from the large selection at the counter. The waitress will then bring it to your table. Coffee is served in cups (**eine Tasse**) or pots (**ein Kännchen**/**eine Portion** = 2 cups). The best time to go to a café is between 3 pm and 5 pm.

- **A typical meal** in a restaurant consists of three courses:
  1. a starter (e.g. soup),
  2. a main course (meat or fish with potatoes and vegetables or salad),
  3. a dessert.

- The restaurants in the large department stores offer reasonably cheap lunches and snacks and quick service.

- **Water** is not served free of charge in German restaurants. Bottled water, which is usually carbonated, must be ordered.

a. Soup **b.** Meat **c.** Poultry, Eggs **d.** Fish

a. die **Suppe** — *soup*

Tagessuppe.	*Soup of the day.*
Tomatensuppe.	*Tomato soup.*
Hühnersuppe.	*Chicken soup.*
Ochsenschwanzsuppe.	*Oxtail soup.*
Gulaschsuppe.	*Goulash soup.*
Nudelsuppe.	*Noodle soup.*

b.

das **Fleisch**	*meat*
das **Rindfleisch**	*beef*
das **Schweinefleisch**	*pork*
das **Kalbfleisch**	*veal*
das **Wild**	*game*
das **Kotelett**	*chop*
das **Schnitzel**	*cutlet*
das **Steak**	*steak*
die **Leber**	*liver*
die **Frikadelle**	*meatball*
der **Schinken**	*ham*
das **Gulasch**	*goulash*
die **Sauce**	*sauce, gravy*

Jägerschnitzel.	*Pork cutlet with spicy mushroom sauce.*
Zigeunerschnitzel.	*Pork cutlet served in spicy sauce with peppers.*
Wiener Schnitzel.	*Breaded veal cutlet.*
Kalbsschnitzel.	*Veal cutlet*
Ein Steak vom Grill.	*Grilled steak.*
Gut durchgebraten, bitte!	*Well-done, please.*
Der gekochte Schinken.	*Boiled ham.*
Der rohe Schinken.	*Smoked ham.*
Eisbein mit Sauerkraut.	*Leg of pork with sauerkraut.*
Hasenpfeffer.	*Hare goulash.*
Rehpfeffer.	*Venison goulash.*
Sauerbraten mit Klößen/ mit Knödel.	*Sliced roast beef, cooked in a special sauce/with dumplings.*

c.

das **Geflügel**	*poultry*
das **Hähnchen**	*chicken*
das **Brathähnchen**	*broiled chicken*
die **Ente**	*duck*
der **Fasan**	*pheasant*
das **Ei**	*egg*
das **Omelett**	*omelette*

Ein halbes Hähnchen, bitte!	*Half a chicken, please.*
Das gekochte Ei.	*Boiled egg.*
Zwei Spiegeleier.	*Two fried eggs.*
Rührei mit Schinken.	*Scrambled eggs with ham.*

d.

der **Fisch**	*fish*
die **Seezunge**	*sole*
die **Scholle**	*plaice*
der **Rotbarsch**	*ocean perch*
der **Kabeljau**	*cod*
der **Hering**	*herring*
die **Krabbe**	*shrimp*
die **Forelle**	*trout*
der **Karpfen**	*carp*

Das Fischfilet.	*Fish fillet.*
Forelle 'blau'.	*Steamed trout.*
Forelle 'Müllerin Art'.	*Trout meunière.*
Krabben-Cocktail	*Shrimp cocktail.*

The waiter comes to take your order. What do you say:

1 If you want chicken soup?

2 If you want a pork cutlet with mushroom sauce?

3 If you want a breaded veal cutlet?

4 If you want a steak – well-done?

5 If you want smoked ham?

6 If you want an omelette?

7 If you want broiled chicken?

8 If you want scrambled eggs with ham?

9 If you want trout meunière?

10   What is being served here?

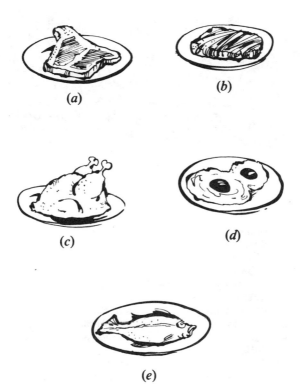

13 Vegetables, Fruit, Desserts

a. Vegetables   **b.** Fruit   **c.** Desserts, Sweets

a.

das	**Gemüse**	*vegetables*
die	**Kartoffeln**	*potatoes*
die	**Erbsen**	*peas*
die	**Bohnen**	*beans*
die	**Karotten, Mohrrüben**	*carrots*
der	**Kohl**/das **Kraut**	*cabbage*
der	**Blumenkohl**	*cauliflower*
das	**Sauerkraut**	*sauerkraut*
der	**Spargel**	*asparagus*
der	**Salat**	*lettuce*
die	**Pilze**	*mushrooms*
die	**Champignons**	*button mushrooms*
die	**Zwiebeln**	*onions*
die	**Gurken**	*cucumbers*
die	**Tomaten**	*tomatoes*
der	**Reis**	*rice*

Salzkartoffeln.	*Boiled potatoes.*
Pellkartoffeln.	*Unpeeled boiled potatoes.*
Bratkartoffeln und Spiegelei.	*Fried eggs and fried potatoes.*
Das Kartoffelpüree.	*Mashed potatoes.*
Grüne Bohnen.	*Runner beans.*

b.

das	**Obst,** die **Früchte**	*fruit*
der	**Apfel**	*apple*
die	**Apfelsine, Orange**	*orange*
die	**Banane**	*banana*
die	**Zitrone**	*lemon*
die	**Himbeeren**	*raspberries*
die	**Erdbeeren**	*strawberries*
die	**Kirsche**	*cherry*
die	**Weintrauben**	*grapes*
die	**Birne**	*pear*
der	**Pfirsich**	*peach*

Ich esse gerne Himbeer-en	*I like raspberries.*
Erdbeeren mit Schlag-sahne.	*Strawberries with whipped cream.*

c.

der	**Kuchen**	*cake*
die	**Torte**	*(layer) cake, fruit tart*
die	**Schlagsahne**	*whipped cream*
der	**Keks**	*biscuit*
die	**Schokolade**	*chocolate*
das	**Konfekt**	*sweets*
das	**Marzipan**	*marzipan*
die	**Praline**	*special chocolate*
das	**Eis**	*ice cream*

Ein Stück Apfelkuchen.	*A piece of apple cake.*
Sahnetorte.	*Cream cake.*
Käsetorte.	*Cheese cake. (without fruit)*
Obsttorte.	*Fruit tart.*
Sachertorte.	*Rich chocolate gateau. (Viennese speciality)*
Schwarzwälder Kirsch-torte.	*Black Forest gateau.*
Vanille-Eis.	*Vanilla ice cream.*
Schokoladeneis.	*Chocolate ice cream.*
Eine Portion Eis mit Sahne, bitte!	*Ice cream with whipped cream, please.*
Einen Eisbecher mit Früchten, bitte!	*A fruit sundae, please.*

13 Vegetables, Fruit, Desserts

What are the following called in German? Say you like them.
Start **Ich esse gerne . . .**
Example: Grüne Bohnen. Ich esse gerne grüne Bohnen.

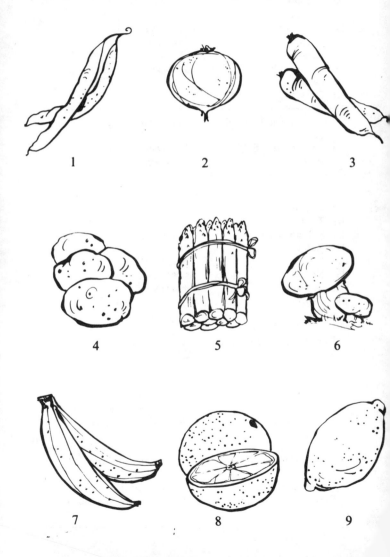

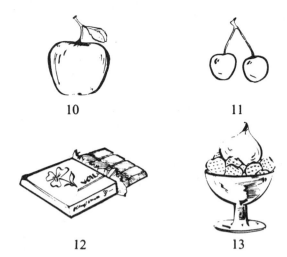

10   11

12   13

- **Potatoes** are prepared in various ways and served with most hot meals.
- When you see the vast array of **cakes** offered in the cafés or when you are invited to a German home, forget about counting calories. These delectable creations of cream, fruit, liqueur and pastry must be tasted to be believed. One of the most delicious **Torten** is the **Schwarzwälder Kirschtorte**, made with chocolate flakes, cherries and kirsch.
- Germany also has a wide assortment of **chocolate** and chocolate sweets.
- The vocabulary in sections 12 and 13 covers most of the basic words to be found on a German menu. Don't be put off by the embellished descriptions of foods and dishes. A closer look will reveal the words you have learnt in this course:

  Petersilien**kartoffeln**, Eifeler Bach**forelle 'blau'**, Butter**reis**, **Spargel**spitzen . . .
- The German fondness for foreign cuisine is reflected in the many Yugoslavian, Italian, Greek and Chinese restaurants to be found in most cities.

a. Non-alcoholic Beverages
b. Alcoholic Beverages   **c.** Smoking

a.	**Getränke**	*drinks, beverages*
	das **Mineralwasser**	*mineral water (usually carbonated)*
	die **Cola**	*cola*
	der **Saft**	*juice*
	der **Kaffee**	*coffee*
	der **Tee**	*tea*
	die **Schokolade**	*hot chocolate, cocoa*
	die **Milch**	*milk*
	die **Buttermilch**	*buttermilk*

Kalte/Warme Getränke.	*Cold/Hot drinks*
Mineralwasser mit/ohne Kohlensäure.	*Carbonated/Non-carbonated mineral water.*
Apfelsaft.	*Apple juice.*
Orangensaft.	*Orange juice.*
Kirschsaft.	*Cherry juice.*
Eine Tasse Kaffee, bitte!	*A cup of coffee, please.*
Ein Kännchen Kaffee, bitte!	*A pot of coffee, please.*
Tee mit Zitrone/mit Milch.	*Tea with lemon/with milk.*

b.

das **Bier**	*beer*
das **Pils**	*lager*
der **Wein**	*wine*
der **Champagner**	*champagne*
der **Sekt**	*sparkling wine*
der **Weinbrand**	*brandy*
der **Korn**	*grain spirit*
der **Schnaps**	*schnapps*
der **Korkenzieher**	*corkscrew*
der **Flaschenöffner**	*bottle-opener*

Einen Schnaps, bitte!	*A schnapps, please.*
Zum Wohle!	*Your health!*
Prost!	*Cheers!*
Rotwein/Weißwein/ Rosé Wein.	*Red wine/White wine/ Rosé wine.*

c.

die **Zigarette**	*cigarette*
die **Zigarre**	*cigar*
die **Pfeife**	*pipe*
der **Tabak**	*tobacco*
das **Feuerzeug**	*lighter*
das **Streichholz**	*match*
der **Aschenbecher**	*ashtray*

Eine Schachtel Zigaretten.	*A packet of cigarettes.*
Zigaretten mit/ohne Filter.	*Filtered/Unfiltered cigarettes.*
Eine Schachtel streichhölzer.	*A box of matches.*
Eine Zigarette rauchen.	*Smoke a cigarette.*
Rauchen verboten!	*No smoking.*

Meals →10

14 Drinking and Smoking

1 The waiter asks if you would like coffee or tea:
Möchten Sie Kaffee oder Tee? You would like tea
with milk, so what do you say?

2 You have ordered a meal in a restaurant. The waiter
asks you what you would like to drink: **Was trinken
Sie?** Say you would like the following items. Start **Ich
möchte** . . . (*I would like* . . .)

(a) an apple juice
(b) a bottle of red wine
(c) a lager
(d) a brandy
(e) a cup of coffee.

3 What are these called in German?

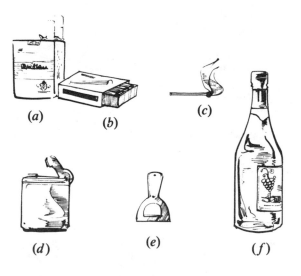

(a) (b) (c) (d) (e) (f)

4 How do you ask for a packet of cigarettes?

5 How do you ask for a box of matches?

Look at this list of beverages.

1 Tasse	**VOLLMER** *Kaffee*	*1,80*
1 Kännchen	**VOLLMER** *Kaffee*	*3,60*
1 Tasse	**KAFFEE HAG**	*1,80*
1 Kännchen	**KAFFEE HAG**	*3,60*
1 Kännchen Mocca		*3,60*
1 Tasse Schokolade mit Sahne		*1,80*
1 Kännchen Schokolade mit Sahne		*3,60*
1 Glas **VOLLMER TEE** mit Milch oder Zitrone		*1,80*
1 Kännchen **VOLLMER TEE** mit Milch oder Zitrone		*3,60*

6 How much is a pot of coffee?

7 How much is a tea with lemon?

- Some interesting statistics: on average, a German drinks an annual 190 litres of coffee, 150 litres of beer, 110 litres of soft drinks, 95 litres of milk, 45 litres of tea, 20 litres of wine, and 16 litres of fruit juice.
- **Breweries** are found in virtually every German city. North German beer has a higher alcohol content than Bavarian beer. **Pils** is a bitter beer, **Export** is slightly sweet. The most famous beer tavern in Germany is the Munich **Hofbräuhaus**.
- Germany is a large producer of **white wines**. Famous wine-growing regions are the Moselle Valley, Rhinehessen, the Nahe, and Baden. German wines are classified as follows (in ascending order of quality): Kabinett, Spätlese, Auslese, Beerenauslese, Trockenbeerenauslese, Eiswein.
- The sale of beer, wine and spirits in restaurants and bars is not restricted to any licensing hours.

a. Tourism **b.** Places of Interest
c. Entertainment **d.** Admission

Heidelberg

a.	die **Reise**	*trip, journey*
	das **Reisebüro**	*travel agency*
	der **Reiseführer**	*travel guide, guidebook*
	der **Reiseleiter**	*tour guide*
	der **Tourist**	*tourist*
	die **Stadtrundfahrt**	*city sightseeing tour*
	der **Prospekt**	*brochure*
b.	die **Sehenswürdigkeiten**	*sights, places of interest*
	die **Kirche**	*church*
	der **Dom**	*cathedral*
	das **Münster**	*minster*
	das **Kloster**	*monastery, convent*
	die **Burg**	*castle, fortress*
	das **Schloß**	*castle, palace*
	das **Tor**	*archway, gate*
	das **Museum**	*museum*

die	**Galerie**	*gallery*
die	**Ausstellung**	*exhibition*
die	**Messe**	*trade fair*

Der Kölner Dom.	*Cologne cathedral.*
Das Heidelberger Schloß.	*Heidelberg castle.*
Das Brandenburger Tor.	*The Brandenburg Gate.*
Das ägyptische Museum in Berlin (mit der Nofretete).	*The Egyptian Museum in Berlin (with Nefertiti).*
Das Deutsche Museum in München.	*The Deutsches Museum in Munich.*
Das Goethehaus in Frankfurt.	*Goethe's house in Frankfurt.*

c.

die	**Veranstaltung**	*event, function*
das	**Theater**	*theatre*
die	**Oper**	*opera*
die	**Konzerthalle**	*concert-hall*
das	**Kino**	*cinema*
das	**Sportstadion**	*sports stadium*
die	**Vorstellung**	*performance*
die	**Eintrittskarte**	*admission ticket*
das	**Parkett**	*orchestra seats, stalls*
der	**1. Rang/2. Rang**	*dress circle/upper circle*
die	**Reihe**	*row*
der	**Sitz**	*seat*

Ich möchte eine Karte für Donnerstag.	*I'd like a ticket for Thursday.*
Wie teuer?	*What price category?*
Etwa für 20 Mark.	*About 20 marks.*
Wann beginnt die Vorstellung?	*What time does the performance start?*

d.

die	**Öffnungszeiten**	*opening times*
	Geöffnet	*open*
	Geschlossen	*closed*
der	**Eingang**	*entrance*
der	**Ausgang**	*exit*
	Drücken	*push*
	Ziehen	*pull*
die	**Garderobe**	*cloakroom*
die	**Führung**	*guided tour*

15   Sightseeing and Entertainment

Do you recognize these tourist attractions? Can you
name them?

1

(Goethe's house)

2

(Brandenburg Gate)

3

(Cologne Cathedral)

4

(Nefertiti)

You visit a museum.

5   Which sign indicates the entrance?

6   Which sign indicates the exit?

7   When you go to the theatre or a museum, where do you check in your coat, umbrella, etc.?

8   If the museum or the shop are closed, what does the sign say?

9   You have been invited to the opera by a friend. Ask him what time the performance starts.

Look at this theatre ticket.

10   In which theatre did the performance take place?

11   In which part of the auditorium did the buyer of this ticket sit?

12   In which row and seat did he sit?

- **Museums** are generally open from 9 am to 5 pm every day except Mondays.
- All cities have **theatres** and concert-halls.
  Most large cities have an opera house too – those in Berlin, Vienna, Hamburg, and Munich are of international standing.
- The Berlin Philharmonic Orchestra and the Vienna Symphony Orchestra are among the best in the world.
- At the theatre and the opera (but not in cinemas) coats, umbrellas, large bags, etc, must be left in the cloakroom. It is not customary to tip usherettes. In the large theatres and opera houses you should wear evening dress.
  In museums, umbrellas and bulky objects must be left in the cloakroom.

16 Excursions and Recreation

a. Excursions **b.** Scenery **c.** Sports
d. Photography

The Black Forest

a.	der **Ausflug**	*excursion, trip*
	die **Rundfahrt**	*sightseeing trip*

Eine Stadtrundfahrt machen.	*Take a city sightseeing tour.*
Der Ausflug ins Gebirge.	*Excursion into the mountains.*

b.	die **See**	*sea, ocean*
	der **See**	*lake*
	die **Insel**	*island*
	der **Strand**	*beach*
	der **Fluß**	*river*
	der **Wald**	*wood, forest*
	der **Park**	*park*
	das **Gebirge**	*mountains, mountain range*
	der **Berg**	*mountain*
	das **Tal**	*valley*

Die Nordsee.	*The North Sea.*
Die Insel Helgoland.	*(The Island of) Helgoland.*
Die Ostsee.	*The Baltic.*
Der Rhein.	*The Rhine*
Der Bodensee.	*Lake Constance.*
Das Mittelgebirge.	*Low mountain range.*
Das Hochgebirge.	*High mountain range.*
Die Alpen.	*The Alps.*
Die Zugspitze.	*The Zugspitze.*

c.

der **Spaziergang**	*walk, stroll*
die **Wanderung**	*hike*
Fußball	*soccer*
Tennis	*tennis*
das **Hallenbad**	*indoor swimming pool*
das **Freibad**	*outdoor swimming pool*
baden, schwimmen	*to bathe, swim*
segeln, Ski laufen	*to sail, ski*
das **Boot**	*boat*
das **Surfbrett**	*surfboard*

Einen Spaziergang machen.	*Take a walk.*
Zum Fußball gehen.	*Go to a football match.*
Fußball spielen.	*Play football.*
Der Bootsverleih.	*Boat hire.*
Ich möchte ein Surfbrett leihen.	*I'd like to hire a surfboard.*

d.

der **Fotoapparat**	*camera*
die **Kamera**	*camera*
der **Film**	*film*
der **Blitz**	*flash*
die **Batterie**	*battery*
das **Foto**	*photo, print*
das **Dia**	*slide*

Einen film für diesen Fotoapparat, bitte!	*A film for this camera, please.*
Einen Film mit 36 Aufnahmen.	*A 36-exposure film.*
Darf man fotografieren?	*May we take photographs?*
Fotografieren verboten!	*No photographs.*

Clothing → 19

16 Excursions and Recreation

What can you see in these pictures? Answer in German starting
Ich sehe ... (*I see* ...).

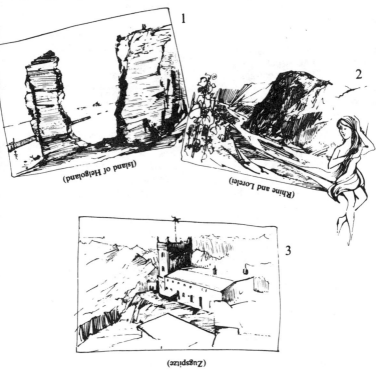

(Island of Helgoland)

(Rhine and Lorelei)

(Zugspitze)

You would like to buy the following items. Ask for them in
German beginning **Ich möchte** ...

4   5   6

What are these sports called in German?

7   8   9

10   Say you would like to hire (*a*) a surfboard;
(*b*) a boat.

- Note that **der See** is a lake (e.g. der Bodensee – Lake Constance) and **die See** is a sea or ocean (e.g. die Nordsee – the North Sea).

- The most important German **tourist areas** are the North Sea, the Baltic, the Harz Mountains, the Rhine between Bingen and Cologne, the Black Forest, the Bavarian Forest, and Upper Bavaria with the Alps. It is advisable to book rooms well in advance if you plan to travel in the peak seasons.

- **Cameras** and **films** of all makes can be bought in Germany at reasonable prices.

- In public **swimming pools** it is usually compulsory to wear a bathing-cap. You can sometimes hire one at the pool.

a. The Weather **b.** Good Weather
c. Bad Weather **d.** Cold Weather

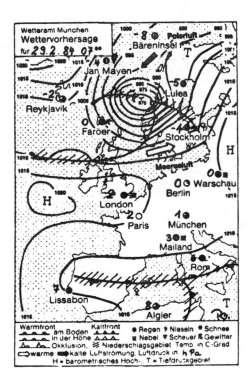

a.

das **Wetter**	weather
der **Wetterbericht**	weather forecast
die **Wetterlage**	weather situation
die **Temperatur**	temperature

Tageshöchsttemperaturen.	*Maximum temperatures.*
Der Temperaturanstieg.	*Rise in temperature.*
Der Temperaturrückgang.	*Fall in temperature.*
Die Aussichten für morgen.	*Outlook for tomorrow.*

b.

das	**schöne Wetter**	*good weather*
	trocken	*dry*
	heiter	*bright, clear*
die	**Aufheiterung**	*clearing up*
die	**Sonne**	*sun*
der	**Sonnenschein**	*sunshine*
	sonnig	*sunny*
	warm	*warm*
	heiß	*hot*
das	**Hoch (H)**	*high-pressure area*

Die Sonne scheint.	*The sun is shining.*
Es ist warm.	*It's warm.*

c.

das	**schlechte Wetter**	*bad weather*
das	**Tief (T)**	*low-pressure area*
die	**Bewölkung**	*clouds*
	wolkig	*cloudy*
	bedeckt	*overcast*
der	**Regen**	*rain*
der	**Niederschlag**	*precipitation*
der	**Schauer**	*shower*
das	**Gewitter**	*thunderstorm*
der	**Regenschirm**	*umbrella*
der	**Wind**	*wind*
der	**Sturm**	*storm*
der	**Nebel**	*fog*

Es regnet.	*It's raining.*
Der Wind ist frisch/ stark/böig.	*There's a fresh/strong/gusty wind.*
Der Westwind.	*West wind.*

d.

	kühl	*cool*
	kalt	*cold*
der	**Schnee**	*snow*
das	**Eis**	*ice*
der	**Frost**	*frost*

Es ist kalt.	*It's cold.*
Es schneit.	*It's snowing.*
Das Glatteis.	*Ice./Icy roads.*

17 The Weather

See how many words you recognise in this weather forecast:

Alpengebiet

In den Tälern stellenweise Frühnebel, sonst aufgelockerte Bewölkung, vielfach sonnig und trocken. Tagestemperaturen um 4 Grad, in 2000 m Höhe um –5 Grad, nachts Frost bis –5 Grad. Auf den Bergen mäßiger Südwestwind.

Deutsches Küstengebiet

Stark diesig, nachts und morgens verbreitet Nebel, tagsüber aufgelockerte Bewölkung, kein Niederschlag. Höchsttemperaturen bis 5 Grad, nachts leichter Frost. Schwacher Wind.

Are the following statements true or false? (Answer **richtig** or **falsch**):

1 In coastal areas there will be morning fog.

2 In coastal areas there will be rain during the day.

3 In the Alps it will be sunny and dry.

4 Maximum temperatures in the Alps will be around 4 degrees.

What do these symbols stand for?

5 ▼   6 ≡   7 ●   8 ＊

What is the weather like?

9

10

- In Germany temperatures are given in **Centigrade** (Celsius). To convert them into Fahrenheit, multiply by 1.8 (or 9/5) and add 32.

°C	−5	0	5	10	15	20	25	30	35
°F	23	32	41	50	59	68	77	86	95

- **Average temperatures** in Germany are around −1° Centigrade (30° F) in winter and 17° Centigrade (63° F) in summer. The highest temperature reached is 38° Centigrade (100° F) in Southwest Germany.

- On average, Germany has 190 rainy days a year. May and September have the lowest **rainfall.** The areas with the highest rainfall are the Alps, the Black Forest and the Harz Mountains.

- The vocabulary in this section is sufficient to enable you to read the weather forecast in a German newspaper.

a. The Post Office   **b.** Letters and Postcards
c. Telephone

a.

die **Post**	post office
der **Briefkasten**	letter-box

Entschuldigen Sie, wo ist die Post?	*Excuse me, where is the post office?*
Deutsche Bundespost.	*German postal service.*

b.

der **Brief**	letter
die **Postkarte**	postcard
die **Adresse**	address
die **Postleitzahl**	post-code
die **Briefmarke**	stamp
der **Absender**	sender
das **Telegramm**	telegram
Luftpost	airmail

Wieviel kostet ein Brief nach England?	*How much is a letter to England?*
Wieviel kostet eine Postkarte nach Kanada?	*How much is a postcard to Canada?*
Zwei Briefmarken zu 80, bitte!	*Two 80 pfennig stamps, please.*

c.

das **Telefon**	telephone
telefonieren	phone, make a phone call
die **Telefonnummer**	telephone number
die **Vorwahl**	area code
das **Telefonbuch**	telephone directory
die **Telefonzelle**	telephone box
die **Auskunft**	operator

Das Ortsgespräch.	*Local call.*
Das Ferngespräch.	*Long distance call.*
Wieviel kostet ein Gespräch nach Edinburgh?	*How much does a call to Edinburgh cost?*
Meine Telefonnummer ist 13 14 48.	*My telephone number is 13 14 48.*
Hallo . . .!	*Hello?*
Bitte warten (Sie).	*Hold the line, please.*
Ruf mal an!	*Give me a ring!*

18 Post Office and Telephone

What are these called in German?

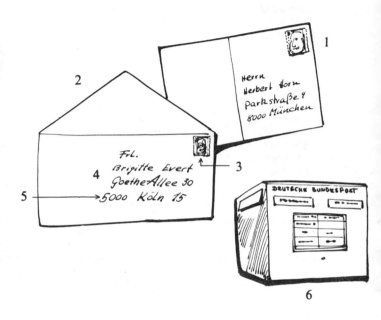

7 You would like to know the postage for a letter to
   Canada. What do you say?

8 You want to buy a stamp for a postcard to England.
   What do you ask for?

9 How do you ask for 3 stamps at 80 pfennigs?

10 How do you say 'long distance call' in German?

11 Give your German friend the number of the hotel
    you are staying at (13 14 48).

12 What is this called in German?

13 If you can't hear a voice at the other end of the line, what do you say?

- **Stamps** may be purchased at the post office and in most shops selling postcards.

- The German **telephone** system allows direct dialling within Germany and to over 100 countries abroad. For international calls from a telephone box, look for the green notice with a black receiver and the words **National – International** or **Inland – Ausland**. To make a phone call, pick up the receiver, insert at least 20 pfennigs (for an international call at least 1 mark) into the slot and dial the number. You will find the list of international codes in every telephone box and you just add your local area code minus the zero to the international code.
  Long distance calls may also be made from the post office. Ask at the counter marked **Ferngespräche**. Telephoning from hotels is three times more expensive (or more) than from public telephone boxes.

  Useful numbers:
directory inquiries (domestic calls)	11	88
(international calls)	001	18
emergency	1	10
fire	1	12

a. Clothing   **b.** Socks and Shoes   **c.** Colours
d. Toiletries   **e.** Hair Care

a.

die	**Kleidung**	*clothes*
der	**Mantel**	*coat*
der	**Hut**	*hat*
der	**Schal**	*scarf*
die	**Jacke**	*jacket*
der	**Anorak**	*anorak*
die	**Hose**	*trousers*
das	**Hemd**	*shirt*
die	**Krawatte**	*tie*
der	**Pullover**	*pullover, sweater*
die	**Bluse**	*blouse*
das	**Kleid**	*dress*
der	**Rock**	*skirt*
die	**Badehose**	*swimming trunks*
der	**Badeanzug**	*swimming costume*
die	**Badekappe**	*bathing cap*

Ich möchte einen Pullover.	*I'd like a pullover.*
Welche Größe?	*What size?*
Wo ist die Anprobe?	*Where is the fitting room?*
Der Pullover ist zu groß/zu klein.	*The pullover is too big/too tight.*

Der Pullover gefällt mir.	*I like the pullover.*
Er gefällt mir nicht.	*I don't like it.*
Ich nehme ihn.	*I'll take it.*

b.

die **Schuhe**	shoes
die **Turnschuhe**	tennis shoes, trainers
die **Stiefel**	boots
die **Socken**	socks
die **Strümpfe**	stockings
die **Strumpfhose**	tights

c.

die **Farben**	colours
weiß, schwarz	white, black
grau, braun	grey, brown
rot, grün	red, green
blau, gelb	blue, yellow

d.

die **Seife**	soap
das **Shampoo**	shampoo
das **Handtuch**	towel
die **Zahnpasta**	toothpaste
die **Zahnbürste**	toothbrush
der **Rasierapparat**	electric razor
die **Rasierklingen**	razor-blades
das **Taschentuch**	handkerchief
die **Damenbinde**	sanitary towel
das **Tampon**	tampon
die **Brille**	glasses

Ein Stück Seife.	*A piece of soap.*
Eine Tube Zahnpasta.	*A tube of toothpaste.*
Die Sonnenbrille.	*Sunglasses.*

e.

die **Haare**	hair
der **Kamm**	comb
der **Friseur**	hairdresser, barber
die **Rasur**	shave

Haare schneiden, bitte.	*Haircut, please.*
Waschen und legen.	*Shampoo and set.*
Föhnen, bitte.	*Blow-dry, please.*

Money, Shopping → 9

19 Clothing and Toiletries

1 You are in a shop and try on the following items.
   What are they called in German?

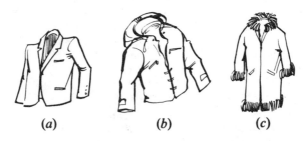

   (a)   (b)   (c)

2 You like the following. Tell the shop assistant so.

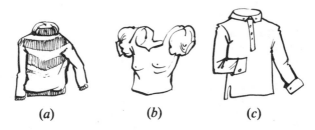

   (a)   (b)   (c)

3 Tell the assistant that the following are too small.

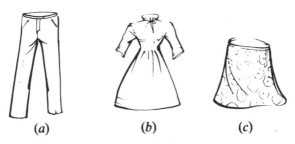

   (a)   (b)   (c)

4 Tell the assistant you would like to buy a shirt.

5 You would like to know where the fitting room is.
   What do you say?

6 The shirt is too big for you. What do you say?

7 You like the shirt and wish to buy it. What do you say?

8 Tell the assistant that the following are too big.

(a)

(b)

(c)

What are these called in German?

9

10

11

– When buying **clothes** or **shoes**, remember that German
  sizes are different from British ones.

Shoe sizes

British	1	2	3	4	5	6	7	8	9	10	11	12
German	33	34–35	36	37	38	39–40	41	42	43	44	45	46

Dress sizes

British	10	12	14	16	18	20
German	38	40	42	44	46	48

Collar sizes

British	13	13½	14	14½	15	15½	16	16½	17
German	33	34	35–36	37	38	39	41	42	43

Suits, coats

British	36	38	40	42	44	46
German	46	48	50	52	54	56

20 Accidents and Emergencies

a. Breakdowns, Accidents **b.** Theft **c.** Police
d. Doctor **e.** Illness **f.** Chemist **g.** Help

a.

die	**Panne**	*breakdown*
der	**Unfall**	*accident*
der	**Verletzte**	*casualty, injured person*
der	**Zeuge**	*witness*
die	**Versicherung**	*insurance*
der	**Automechaniker**	*mechanic*
die	**Werkstatt**	*repair garage*

Mein Auto springt nicht an.	*My car won't start.*
Der Sachschaden.	*Material damage.*
Der Personenschaden.	*Injury.*
Ort, Datum und Zeit des Unfalls.	*Place, date and time of the accident.*
Die Versicherungskarte.	*Insurance card.*
Einen Unfall melden.	*Report an accident.*

b.

die	**Wertgegenstände**	*valuables*
der	**Hotelsafe**	*hotel safe*
	verloren	*lost*
	gestohlen	*stolen*
das	**Portemonnaie**	*purse*
die	**Brieftasche**	*wallet*

Ich habe den Schlüssel verloren.	*I've lost the key.*
Mir ist der Fotoapparat gestohlen worden.	*My camera has been stolen.*

c.

die	**Polizei (-wache)**	*police (-station)*
der	**Polizist**	*policeman*
die	**Geldstrafe**	*fine*
der	**Rechtsanwalt**	*lawyer*

Rufen Sie bitte die Polizei!	*Call the police, please!*
Anzeige erstatten.	*Bring a charge against someone.*

d.

der **Arzt**	*doctor*
der **Zahnarzt**	*dentist*
das **Krankenhaus**	*hospital*
der **Krankenwagen**	*ambulance*

Rufen Sie einen Arzt!	*Call a doctor!*
Der ärztliche Notdienst.	*Medical emergency service.*
Erste Hilfe.	*First aid.*

e.

krank	*sick, ill*
das **Fieber**	*fever*
der **Herzanfall**	*heart attack*

Ich habe Kopfschmerzen.	*I have a headache.*
Ich habe Magenschmerzen.	*I have a stomachache.*
Ich kann nicht schlafen.	*I can't sleep.*
Ich habe Fieber.	*I have a temperature.*
Ich habe mich verletzt.	*I've hurt myself.*
Ich habe Zahnschmerzen.	*I have toothache.*
Ich habe mir den Finger verbrannt.	*I have burnt my finger.*
Ich habe mir den Fuss verletzt.	*I have hurt my foot.*

f.

die **Apotheke**	*chemist, pharmacy*
die **Tablette**	*pill*
die **Rezept**	*prescription*
das **Pflaster**	*sticking-plaster*

Ich brauche Schlaftabletten.	*I need some sleeping pills.*
Ich brauche Tabletten gegen Kopfschmerzen.	*I need something for a headache.*

g.

die **Gefahr**	*danger*
Achtung!	*Caution! (on a sign)/Watch out!*

Hilfe!	*Help!*
Vorsicht!	*Careful!*
Notausgang.	*Emergency Exit.*

20   Accidents and Emergencies

1   You are telephoning a garage. Tell the mechanic your car won't start.

2   You are involved in an accident. How do you ask someone to call the police?

3   Say you would like to report an accident. What do you say to the police?

4   Tell the police you have lost your passport.

5   Say that someone has stolen your wallet.

6   You have witnessed an accident. How do you tell someone to call an ambulance?

7   You go to a doctor. Tell him:
    (a) you have a temperature;
    (b) you have burnt your hand;
    (c) you have hurt your foot.

8   Tell the chemist you need
    (a) some sleeping pills;
    (b) something for a stomachache;
    (c) some sticking-plasters.

9   Tell the dentist you have toothache.

- In case of **breakdown** on the Autobahn there are arrows on the crash barriers indicating which way to walk to the nearest telephone. The recovery service is organised by the German Automobile Club (**Allgemeiner Deutscher Automobil Club**). The emergency phone number is 1 10, and for fire 1 12.

- If you are caught **breaking a speed limit,** you have to produce a valid driving licence and you may be fined on the spot by the police officer according to German law. This avoids lengthy procedures at the police station.

- If you have been stopped under suspicion of having drunk too much alcohol, you may be **breathalysed** and if a further blood-test is required you will have to go to the nearest police station. If you are found to be over the limit you will not be allowed to continue your journey and your licence will be impounded.

- **Health Service** There is a reciprocal agreement between West Germany and the UK whereby money paid out in doctor's and hospital fees can usually be recovered on return to the UK. Remember to obtain form E111 in advance of your visit.

- All **chemists** are well qualified to advise on any general medical matter and will produce the appropriate medicine or they can provide the name and address of a doctor on call. If the chemist is closed (Sunday or Public Holiday) you will find a notice on the door giving the address of the duty chemist.

Here are some names of **parts of the body** in German:

der Kopf *head*	**die Hand** *hand*
die Ohren *ears*	**der Arm** *arm*
die Augen *eyes*	**die Brust** *chest*
die Lippen *lips*	**das Bein** *leg*
die Nase *nose*	**das Knie** *knee*
der Hals *throat*	**der Fuß** *foot*

Ich habe Halsschmerzen.   *I have a sore throat.*
Ich habe Ohrenschmerzen.   *I have earache.*

Answers

1 General Expressions
1 Der Koffer. 2 Die Handtasche. 3 Guten Morgen, Frau Miller. 4 Guten Tag! 5 Sind Sie Frau Jackson? 6 Ja, ich bin Frau Jackson. 7 Ist das Ihr Koffer? 8 Nein. 9 Bitte schön. 10 Danke schön. 11 Guten Abend, Herr Schmidt. 12 Wie geht's? 13 Danke, gut! 14 Meine Frau. 15 Auf Wiedersehen, Herr Schmidt.

2 Arriving in Germany
1 Der Reisepaß. 2 Der Führerschein. 3 Nein. 4 Machen Sie bitte den Koffer auf. 5 Paßkontrolle. 6 Ihren Ausweis, bitte/ Ihre Reisepaß, bitte. 7 Ja, ich bin Engländer/Engländerin. 8 Ich verstehe nicht. 9 Haben Sie eine englische Zeitung? 10 Groß Britannien. 11 Australien. 12 (Bundesrepublik) Deutschland.

3 Driving a Car
1 Der PKW, das Auto. 2 Der Wohnwagen. 3 Das Fahrrad. 4 Autovermietung. 5 Wieviel? 6 Voll, bitte! 7 Bitte den Ölstand prüfen. 8 Dreißig Liter Super, bitte. 9 Autobahn. 10 Tankstelle. 11 Parkplatz. 12 Autobahn nach Berlin. 13 Ausfahrt. 14 (a) Autobahndreieck. (b) Autobahnkreuz.

4 Finding Your Way
1 Norden, Süden, Osten, Westen. 2 Einen Stadtplan von Bonn, bitte. 3 Eine Straßenkarte von Süddeutschland, bitte. 4 Zentrum. 5 Wo ist das Rathaus, bitte? 6 Geradeaus fahren. 7 Nach rechts abbiegen. 8 Nach links abbiegen. 9 Geradeaus. 10 Links.

5 Public Transport
1 U-Bahn. 2 S-Bahn. 3 Hallo Taxi! 4 Zum Flughafen, bitte. 5 Zum Hauptbahnhof, bitte. 6 Auskunft. 7 Fahrplan (or Auskunft). 8 Fahrkarten. 9 Intercity Zug. 10 Eine Rückfahrkarte. 11 Einmal München, bitte. 12 Bitte gehen Sie zum Ausgang 5.

6 Accommodation
1 Das Bett. 2 Der Schlüssel. 3 Ich suche ein Hotel. 4 Ich möchte ein Einzelzimmer, bitte. 5 Ich möchte ein Doppelzimmer, bitte. 6 Für eine Nacht. 7 Ein Zimmer mit Dusche ist frei. 8 Ich möchte ein Zimmer mit Bad. 9 Wieviel kostet das Zimmer? 10 Ich möchte bezahlen./Die Rechnung bitte. 11 Wo ist die Toilette, bitte? 12 Wo ist der Campingplatz, bitte? 13 Wo ist die Jugendherberge, bitte?

7 Numbers, Weights and Measures

1 Fünfzehn. 2 Siebenundzwanzig. 3 Hundertzehn. 4 Zwei-hund ertdreizehn. 5 Zwei Mark. 6 (a) hundertneunzig Kilometer; (b) vierhundert Kilometer; (c) zweihundertneunzig Kilometer; (d) hundertfünfzig Kilometer; (e) hundertdreißig Kilometer; (f) hundertvierzig Kilometer. 7 Ein Pfund or fünfhundert Gramm. 8 Ein halber Liter. 9 Tausend Gramm. 10 Ein halbes Pfund or zweihundert fünfzig Gramm.

8 Times and Dates

1 (a) eine Stunde; (b) eine halbe Stunde; (c) der Morgen; Vormittag; (d) der Nachmittag; (e) die Nacht. 2 (a) ein Tag; (b) eine Woche. 3 Wieviel Uhr ist es? 4 (a) es ist zehn Uhr. (b) es ist Viertel nach zehn. (c) es ist halb elf. (d) es ist Viertel vor elf. (e) es ist drei Uhr. (f) es ist sechs Uhr. 5 Acht Uhr vierunddreißig. 6 Elf Uhr einundzwanzig. 7 Acht Uhr dreiundvierzig. 8 Neunzehn Uhr vierzehn. 9 Er kommt um neunzehn Uhr an. 10 Wann fährt der Autobus ab?

9 Money and Shopping

1 Wechselstube/Bank. 2 Ich möchte fünfzig Pfund eintauschen. 3 Ich möchte mich nur umsehen. 4 Ich möchte einen Koffer (kaufen). 5 Wieviel kostet er? 6 Sonst noch etwas? 7 Danke, das ist alles. 8 Ich möchte mit Kreditkarte bezahlen. 9 Die Fußgängerzone. 10 Hertie. 11 Berlin. 12 Eine Mark achtunddreißig. 13 Drei Mark achtundneunzig. 14 Fünf Mark sechsunddreißig.

10 Meals

1 (a) das Frühstück; (b) das Mittagessen; (c) das Abendessen. 2 (a) die Tasse; (b) die Gabel; (c) der Teller; (d) das Messer; (e) der Löffel; (f) das Glas; (g) die Flasche. 3 (a) eine Scheibe Brot; (b) das Brot; (c) das Brötchen; (d) die Wurst; (e) der Käse; (e) das Ei. 4 Ich möchte ein Zimmer mit Vollpension. 5 Eine Tasse Tee, bitte. 6 Eine Tasse Kaffee mit Milch, bitte. 7 Eine Scheibe Toastbrot mit Butter und Konfitüre, bitte. 8 Eine Bratwurst mit Kartoffelsalat, bitte. 9 Ein Glas Wein, bitte. 10 Würstchen mit Pommes Frites, bitte.

11 Restaurants

1 (a) das Restaurant; (b) das Café; (c) die Weinstube. 2 Einen Tisch für 3 (Personen) bitte. 3 Entschuldigen Sie, ist dieser Platz noch frei? 4 Nein, er ist besetzt. 5 Nein. 6 Die Speisekarte bitte. 7 Was trinken Sie?/Was möchten Sie trinken? 8 Einen

Apfelsaft, bitte. 9 Die Rechnung, bitte. 10 Zusammen.
11 Stimmt so. 12 (a) das Salz; (b) der Pfeffer; (c) der Senf.

12 Soup, Meat, Fish
1 Hühnersuppe, bitte. 2 Ein Jägerschnitzel, bitte. 3 Ein Wiener
Schnitzel, bitte. 4 Ein Steak, gut durchgebraten, bitte.
5 Rohen Schinken, bitte. 6 Ein Omelett, bitte.
7 Brathähnchen, bitte. 8 Rührei mit Schinken, bitte.
9 Forelle 'Müllerin Art', bitte. 10 (a) ein Kotelett; (b) ein Steak;
(c) ein Hähnchen; (d) zwei Spiegeleier; (e) ein Fisch.

13 Vegetables, Fruit, Desserts
1 Grüne Bohnen. Ich esse gerne grüne Bohnen. 2 Zwiebeln. Ich
esse gerne Zwiebeln. 3 Karotten. Ich esse gerne Karotten (or
Mohrrüben). 4 Kartoffeln. Ich esse gerne Kartoffeln. 5 Spargel.
Ich esse gerne Spargel. 6 Pilze. Ich esse gerne Pilze. 7 Bananen.
Ich esse gerne Bananen. 8 Apfelsinen. Ich esse gerne Apfelsinen (or
Orangen). 9 Zitronen. Ich esse gerne Zitronen. 10 Äpfel. Ich
esse gerne Äpfel. 11 Kirschen. Ich esse gerne Kirschen.
12 Schokolade. Ich esse gerne Schokolade. 13 Erdbeeren
mit Schlagsahne. Ich esse gerne Erdbeeren mit Schlagsahne.

14 Drinking and Smoking
1 Tee mit Milch, bitte. 2 (a) Ich möchte einen Apfelsaft; (b) Ich
möchte eine Flasche Rotwein; (c) Ich möchte ein Pils; (d) Ich
möchte einen Weinbrand; (e) Ich möchte eine Tasse Kaffee.
3 (a) die Schachtel Zigaretten; (b) die Schachtel Streichhölzer;
(c) das Streichholz; (d) das Feuerzeug; (e) der Flaschenöffner;
(f) die Flasche Wein. 4 Eine Schachtel Zigaretten, bitte.
5 Eine Schachtel Streichölzer, bitte. 6 Drei Mark sechzig.
7 Eine Mark achtzig.

15 Sightseeing and Entertainment
1 Das Goethehaus. 2 Das Brandenburger Tor. 3 Der Kölner
Dom. 4 Nofretete. 5 Eingang. 6 Ausgang. 7 Garderobe.
8 Geschlossen. 9 Wann beginnt die Vorstellung? 10 Deutsche
Oper Berlin. 11 Parkett. 12 Reihe 17, Sitz Nr. 11.

16 Excursions and Recreation
1 Ich sehe die Insel Helgoland. 2 Ich sehe den Rhein und die
Lorelei. 3 Ich sehe die Zugspitze. 4 Segeln. 5 Tennis.
6 Fußball. 7 Ich möchte eine Kamera/einen Fotoapparat.
8 Ich möchte einen Film. 9 Ich möchte einen Blitz.
10 (a) Ich möchte ein Surfbrett leihen. (b) Ich möchte ein Boot
leihen.

17 The Weather

1 Richtig. 2 Falsch. 3 Richtig. 4 Richtig. 5 Schauer.
6 Nebel. 7 Regen. 8 Schnee. 9 Es regnet/Der Wind ist
stark. 10 Es ist warm/Die Sonne scheint.

18 Post Office and Telephone

1 Die Postkarte. 2 Der Brief. 3 Die Briefmarke. 4 Die
Adresse. 5 Die Postleitzahl. 6 Der Briefkasten. 7 Wieviel
kostet ein Brief nach Kanada? 8 Eine Briefmarke für eine
Postkarte nach England, bitte. 9 Drei Briefmarken zu achtzig,
bitte. 10 Das Ferngespräch. 11 Meine Telefonnummer ist
dreizehn–vierzehn–achtundvierzig. 12 Das Telefon. 13 Hallo?

19 Clothing and Toiletries

1 (a) die Jacke; (b) der Anorak; (c) der Mantel. 2 (a) Der
Pullover gefällt mir. (b) Die Bluse gefällt mir. (c) Das Hemd
gefällt mir. 3 (a) Die Hose ist zu klein. (b) Das Kleid ist zu
klein. (c) Der Rock ist zu klein. 4 Ich möchte ein Hemd. 5 Wo
ist die Anprobe? 6 Das Hemd ist zu groß. 7 Das Hemd gefällt
mir. Ich nehme es. 8 (a) Die Schuhe sind zu groß. (b) Die Stiefel
sind zu groß. (c) Die Strumpfhose ist zu groß. 9 Die
Zahnbürste. 10 Die Zahnpasta. 11 Der Kamm.

20 Accidents and Emergencies

1 Mein Auto springt nicht an. 2 Rufen Sie bitte die Polizei!
3 Ich möchte einen Unfall melden. 4 Ich habe meinen Reisepaß
verloren. 5 Mir ist die Brieftasche gestohlen worden.
6 Rufen Sie einen Krankenwagen! 7 (a) ich habe Fieber;
(b) ich habe mir die Hand verbrannt; (c) ich habe mir den Fuß
verletzt. 8 (a) ich brauche Schlaftabletten; (b) ich brauche
Tabletten gegen Magenschmerzen; (c) ich brauche Pflaster. 9 Ich
habe Zahnschmerzen.

German-English Vocabulary

abbiegen to turn 4d
Abend evening 8b
Abendbrot supper 10a
Abendessen supper, dinner 10a
abfahren to leave, depart 8b
Abfahrt departure 5e
abreisen to leave 8b
Achtung caution, danger 20g
Adresse address 2b/18b
Allee avenue 4c
Ampel traffic light(s) 4c
Ankunft arrival 5e
Anlegestelle docking area 5c
ankommen to arrive 8b
anmelden to declare 2a
Anorak anorak 19a
Anprobe fitting room 19a
Apfel apple 13b
Apfelsaft apple juice 11b
Apfelsine orange 13b
Apotheke chemist 20e
Arzt doctor 20f
Aschenbecher ash tray 14c
Aufheiterung clearing up 17b
aufmachen to open 2a
Auf Wiedersehen goodbye 1b
Augenblick moment 8a
Ausfahrt exit 3b
Ausflug excursion, trip 16a
Ausgang exit 5b/15d, gate 5b
Auskunft information, telephone 5e, operator 18c
Ausländer(in) foreigner 2c
Ausstellung exhibition 15b
Australien Australia 2c
Australier, Australierin Australian 2c
Ausweis identity card 2b
Auto car 3a
Autobahn motorway 3b
Autobahndreieck motorway junction 3b
Autobahnkreuz motorway intersection 3b
Autobus bus 5d
Autofahrer driver 3a
Autovermietung car hire 3a
Automechaniker mechanic 20a

Bad bath 6b
Badehose swimming trunks 19a
Badeanzug swimming costume 19a
Badekappe bathing cap 19a
baden to swim, bathe 16c
Bahnhof railway station 5a
Banane banana 13b
Bank bank 9b
bar bezahlen to pay in cash 9d
Batterie battery 16d
bedeckt overcast 17c
Benzin petrol 3c
Berg mountain 16b
besetzt occupied 6d; taken 11a
bestellen to order 11b
Bett bed 6b
Bewölkung clouds 17c
bezahlen to pay 3d/9d
Bier beer 14b
billig cheap 9d
Birne pear 13b
bitte please 1c
blau blue 19c
bleifrei lead free 3c
Blitz flash 16d
Blumenkohl cauliflower 13a
Bluse blouse 19a
Bockwurst frankfurter sausage 10b
Bohnen beans 13a
böig gusty 17c
Boot boat 16c
Bootsverleih boat hire 16c
Bordkarte boarding card 5b
Botschaft embassy 2c
Brathähnchen broiled chicken 12c
braun brown 19c
Brief letter 18b
Briefkasten postbox 18a
Briefmarke stamp 18b
Brieftasche wallet 20b
Brille glasses 19d
britisch British 2c
Brot bread 10c
Brötchen roll 10c
Brücke bridge 4c
buchen to book 5b/15a

German-English Vocabulary

Bundesrepublik Deutschland Federal Republic of Germany 2c
Bundesstraße major road 3b
Burg castle, fortress 15b
Bushaltestelle bus stop 5d
Butter butter 10c
Buttermilch buttermilk 14a

Café café 11a
Campingplatz campsite 6a
Champagner Champagne 14b
Champignons button mushrooms 13a

Dame lady 1d
Damen ladies 6d
Damenbinde sanitary towel 19d
Damm embankment 4c
danke thanks 1c
das the 1e
Datum date 20a
Deck deck 5c
dein your 1f
der the 1e
deutsch German 2c
Deutsche German (man, woman) 2c
Deutsche Bundesbahn German federal railways 5a
Deutsche Demokratische Republik German Democratic Republic 2c
Deutschland Germany 2c
Dia slide 16d
die the 1e
Dienstag Tuesday 8c
Diesel diesel 3c
Dom cathedral 15b
Donnerstag Thursday 8c
Doppelzimmer double room 6b
Dorf village 4b
Drogerie drugstore 20e
drücken to push 15d
du you 1f
Dusche shower 6b
D-Zug express train 5a

Ei egg 10c/12c
Eilzug express train 5a
ein a 1e
Einbahnstraße one-way street 4c
Eingang entrance 15d
Einkaufszentrum shopping centre 9c
eintauschen to change 9b
Eintrittskarte admission ticket 15c
Einzelzimmer single room 6b
Eis ice cream 13c; ice 17d
Eisenbahn railway 5a
England England 2c
Engländer Englishman 2c
Engländerin Englishwoman 2c
english English 2c
Ente duck 12c
Entschuldigen Sie excuse me 1c
Erbsen peas 13a
Erdbeere strawberry 13b
Erdgeschoß ground floor, main floor 6b
Erste Hilfe first aid 20f
essen to eat 10a
Essig vinegar 11c

Fähre ferry 5c
fahren to ride, drive 3a
Fahrkarte ticket 5e
Fahrplan timetable 5e
Fahrpreis fare 5e
Fahrrad bicycle 3a
Fahrstuhl lift 6b
Farbe colour 19c
Fasan pheasant 12c
Ferngespräch long distance call 18c
Feuerzeug lighter 14c
Fieber fever 20d
Fisch fish 12d
Fischfilet fish fillet 12d
Flasche bottle 10b
Flaschenöffner bottle opener 14b
Fleisch meat 12b
Flug flight 5b
Flughafen airport 5b
Flugschein air ticket 5b
Fluß river 16b
föhnen to blow-dry 19e

German-English Vocabulary

Forelle trout 12d
Foto photo, print 16d
Fotoapparat camera 16d
Frau woman, Mrs, 1d, wife 1f
Fräulein young lady 1d; waitress 11d
frei vacant 6d
Freibad outdoor swimming pool 16c
Freitag Friday 8c
Frikadelle meatball 12b
frisch fresh 17c
Friseur hairdresser, barber 19e
Früchte fruit 13b
Frühstück breakfast 10a
Führerschein driving licence 2b
Führung guided tour 15d
Fußball soccer 16c
Fußgänger pedestrian 4c
Fußgängerzone pedestrian shopping precinct 4c/9c

Gabel fork 10b
Galerie gallery 15b
Gang course 11b
Garage garage 3d
Garderobe cloakroom 15d
Gasse narrow street 4c
Gast guest 11a
Gebirge mountains, mountain range 16b
gebührenpflichtig subject to charge 3d
Gedeck cover (charge) 11b
Gefahr danger 20g
Geflügel poultry 12c
gehen to go 5b
gekocht boiled 12b
gelb yellow 19c
Geld money 9a
Geldstrafe fine 20c
Gemüse vegetables 13a
geöffnet open 15d
Gepäck luggage 2a
geradeaus straight ahead 4d
Geschäft shop store 9c
geschlossen closed 15d
gestern yesterday 8b
gestohlen stolen 20b
Getränke drinks, beverages 14a

Gewitter thunderstorm 17c
Glas glass 10b
Glatteis icy roads, ice 17d
Gleis track, platform 5a
Gramm gram 7b
grau grey 19c
groß big 19a
Großbritannien Great Britain 2c
Größe size 19a
Großstadt city 4b
grün green 19c
Gulasch goulash 12b
Gulaschsuppe goulash soup 12a
Gurken cucumbers 13a
Guten Abend good evening 1b
Gute Nacht good night 1b
Guten Appetit bon appétit 11b
Guten Morgen good morning 1b
Guten Tag good morning, good afternoon, hello 1b

Haare hair 19e
Hafen harbour, port 5c
Hähnchen chicken 12c
Halbpension room with breakfast and 1 main meal 10a
Hallenbad indoor swimming pool 16c
Hallo hello 1b/18c
Handtasche handbag 1e/f
Handtuch towel 19d
Hauptbahnhof main station 5a
Hauptstraße main street 4c
heiß hot 17b
heissen to be called 1d
heiter bright, clear 17b
helfen to help 9c
Hering herring 12d
Herr gentleman, Mr 1d
Herren gentlemen 6d
Herzanfall heart attack 20d
heute today 8b
Hilfe help 20g
Himbeeren raspberries 13b
Hoch high pressure area 17b
Hose trousers 19a
Hotel hotel 6a
Hotelsafe hotel safe 20b

German-English Vocabulary

Hühnersuppe chicken soup 12a
Hut hat 19a

ich I 1f
Ihr your 1f
Imbiß quick bite, snack 10d
Imbißstube snack bar 10d
Information information (desk) 5e
Innenstadt city centre 4b
Insel island 16b
Intercity-Zug express train 5a

ja yes 1a
Jacke jacket 19a
Jahr year 8c
jeden Tag every day 8b
Jugendherberge youth hostel 6a
Junge boy 1d

Kabeljau cod 12d
Kabine cabin 5c
Kaffee coffee 10c/14a
Kaffeekanne coffeepot 10b
Kalbfleisch veal 12b
kalt cold 14a/17d
Kamera camera 16d
Kamm comb 19e
Kanada Canada 2c
Kanadier(in) Canadian (man, woman) 2c
kanadisch Canadian 2c
Kännchen pot 14a
Kanne coffeepot, tea pot 10b
Karpfen carp 12d
Kartoffeln potatoes 13a
Kartoffelsalat potato salad 10d
Käse cheese 10c
Kasse cashier, cash register 9d
Kassenbon cash register receipt 9d
kaufen buy 9c
Kaufhaus department store 9c
Keks biscuit 13c
Kellner water 11d
Ketchup ketchup 10d
Kilo kilogram 7b
Kilometer kilometre 7b

Kino cinema 15c
Kirche church 15b
Kirsche cherry 13b
Kleid dress 19a
Kleidung clothing 19a
klein tight 19a
Kleingeld change 9a
Kleinstadt town 4b
Kloster monastery, convent 15b
Koffer suitcase 2a
Kofferraum boot (of car) 2a
Kohl cabbage 13a
Konfekt sweets 13c
Konfiture jam 10c
Konzerthalle concert-hall 15c
Konsulat consulate 2c
Kopfschmerzen headache 20d
Korkenzieher cork screw 14b
Korn grain spirit 14b
kosten to cost 9d
Kotelett chop 12b
Krabbe shrimp 12d
krank sick, ill 20d
Krankenhaus hospital 20f
Krankenwagen ambulance 20f
Kraut cabbage 13a
Krawatte tie 19a
Kreditkarte credit-card 9b
Kuchen cake 13c
kuhl cool 17d
Kunde customer 9c
Kurswagen through coach 5a

Landkarte map 4a
Landstraße secondary road 3b
langsam slowly 4
Lastkraftwagen truck 3a
Lebensmittel groceries 9
Leber liver 12b
leid : es tut mir leid I'm sorry 1c
leihen to hire 16c
Liegewagen couchette 5a
Linie line 5d
links (to the) left 4d
Liter litre 7b
LKW lorry 3a
Löffel spoon 10b
Luftpost airmail 18b

German-English Vocabulary

Mädchen girl 1d
Magenschmerzen stomachache 20d
Mann husband 1f
Mantel coat 19a
Mark mark 9a
Markt market 9c
Marzipan marzipan 13c
mehr more 7b
Mehrwertsteuer VAT 9d
mein my 1f
melden to report 20a
Messe trade fair 15b
Messer knife 10b
Meter metre 7b
Milch milk 14a
Mineralwasser mineral water 14a
Minute minute 8a
Mittag midday 8b
Mittagessen lunch 10a
Mitternacht midnight 8b
Mittwoch Wednesday 8c
Möhren carrots 13a
Mohrrüben carrots 13a
Monat month 8c
Montag Monday 8c
Moped small motorcycle 3a
Morgen morning, tomorrow 8b
Motorrad motorcycle 3a
Munster minster 15b
Museum museum 15b

Nachmittag afternoon 8b
nächste woche next week 8c
Nacht night 8b
Nachtisch dessert 11b
Nahverkehrszug local commuter train 5a
Name name 2b
Nebel fog 17c
nehmen to take 19a
nein no 1a
Niederschlag precipitation 17c
Norddeutschland Northern Germany 4a
Norden north 4d
Normal 2-star 3c
Notausgang emergency exit 20f
Notdienst emergency service 20f

Nudelsuppe noodle soup 12a

Ober (head) waiter 11d
Oberhemd shirt 19a
Obst fruit 13b
Ochsenschwanzsuppe oxtail soup 12a
Öffnungszeiten opening times 15d
Öl oil 3c
Ölwechsel oil change 3c
Omelett omelette 12c
Oper opera 15c
Orangensaft orange juice 10c
Ort place 20a
Ortsgespräch local call 18c
Osten east 4d
Österreich Austria 2c

Paar pair 19b
Panne breakdown 20a
Park park 16b
parken to park 3d
Parkett orchestra seats 15c
Parkgebuhr parking fee 3d
Parkhaus parking garage 3d
Parkplatz parking spot, car park 3d
Parkscheibe parking disc 3d
Parkuhr parking metre 3d
Paßkontrolle passport control 2b
Pension guest house 6a
Personenschaden injury 20a
Personenkraftwagen car 3a
Pfeffer pepper 11c
Pfeife pipe 14c
Pfennig pfennig 9a
Pfirsich peach 13b
Pflaster sticking plaster 20e
Pfund pound 7b
Pils pils 14b
Pilze mushrooms 13a
Pkw car 3a
Platz square 4c, seat 11a
Platzreservierung seat reservation 5e
Polizei police(-station) 20c
Polizist policeman 20c
Pommes frites chips 10d

German-English Vocabulary

Portemonnaie purse 20b
Post post office 18a
Postkarte postcard 18b
Postleitzahl post code 18b
Praline chocolate sweet 13c
Preis price 6c/9d
Privatzimmer room rented in a private home 6a
Prospekt brochure 15a
Prost cheers 14b
prüfen to check 3c
Pullover pullover, sweater 19a

Quittung receipt 9d

Rang balcony 15c
Rasierapparat electric razor 19d
Rasierklingen razor-blades 19d
Raststätte rest stop 3b
Rasur shave 19e
Rathaus town hall 4b
rauchen to smoke 14c
Rechnung bill 6c, 11d
rechts (to the) right 4d
Rechtsanwalt lawyer 20c
Regen rain 17c
Regenschirm umbrella 17c
regnen to rain 17c
Reifen tyre 3c
Reihe row 5b/15c
Reis rice 13a
Reise trip, journey 15a
Reisebüro travel agency 15a
Reiseführer travel guide, guidebook 15a
Reiseleiter tour guide 15a
Reisepaß passport 2b
Reisescheck traveller's cheque 9b
reserviert reserved 6b, 11a
Restaurant restaurant 11a
Rezeption reception (desk) 6b
Richtung direction 4d
Rindfleisch beef 12b
Rock skirt 19a
Rollsplitt gravel 3b
rot red 19c
Rotbarsch ocean perch 12d

Rückfahrkarte return ticket 5e
rufen to call 20c
Ruhrei scrambled eggs 12c
Rundfahrt sightseeing trip 16a

Sachschaden material damage 20a
Saft juice 14a
Salz salt 11c
Samstag Saturday 8c
Sauce sauce 12b
Sauce gravy 12b
Sauerkraut sauerkraut 13a
S-Bahn suburban railway 5d
Schachtel packet 14c
Schal scarf 19a
Schauer shower 17c
Scheck cheque 9d
Scheibe slice 10c
scheinen to shine 17b
Schein (bank) note 9a
Schiff ship 5c
Schinken ham 12b
schlafen to sleep 20b
Schlaftablette sleeping pill 20e
Schlafwagen sleeping car 5a
Schlagsahne whipped cream 13c
schlecht bad 17c
Schließfach luggage locker 5e
Schlüssel key 6b
Schnaps schnapps 14b
Schnee snow 17d
schneien to snow 17d
Schnellbahn suburban railway 5d
Schnitzel cutlet 12b
Schokolade chocolate 13c; hot chocolate, cocoa 14a
Scholle plaice 12d
schönes Wetter good weather 17b
Schotte, Schottin Scotsman, Scotswoman 2c
Schuhe shoes 19b
schwarz black 19c
Schweinefleisch pork 12b
Schweiz Switzerland 2c
schwimmen to swim 16c
See sea, ocean, lake 16b
Seezunge sole 12d

German-English Vocabulary

segeln to sail 16c
Sehenswurdigkeiten sights 15b
Seife soap 19d
Sekt sparkling-wine 14b
Selbstbedienung self service 11a
Senf mustard 10d
Shampoo shampoo 19d
Sicherheitskontrolle security check 5b
Sie you 1f
Sitz seat 5b/15c
Ski laufen to ski 16c
Socken socks 19b
Sonderangebot sale item 9c
Sonne sun 17b
Sonnenbrille sunglasses 19d
Sonnenschein sunshine 17b
sonnig sunny 17b
Sonntag Sunday 8c
Spargel asparagus 13a
Sparkasse savings and loan association 9b
Spaziergang walk, stroll 16c
Speisekarte menu 11b
Staatsangehörigkeit nationality 2c
Stadt city 4b
Stadtplan street/town map 4a
Stadtrundfahrt city sightseeing tour 15a
stark strong 17c
Stau traffic jam 3b
Steak steak 12b
Stiefel boots 19b
Stockwerk floor 6b
Strand beach 16b
Straße street 4c
Straßenkarte road map 4a
Streichholz match 14c
Strümpfe stockings 19b
Strumpfhose tights 19b
Stück piece 19d
Stunde hour 8a
Sturm storm 17c
Süden south 4d
Super 4-star 3c
Supermarkt supermarket 9c
Suppe soup 12a
Surfbrett surfboard 16c

Tabak tobacco 14c
Tablette pill 20e
Tag day 8b
Tagesmenü menu of the day 11b
Tagessuppe soup of the day 12a
Tal valley 16b
Tampon tampon 19d
tanken to buy petrol 3c
Tankstelle petrol station 3c
Tasche bag 2a
Taschentuch handkerchief 19d
Tasse cup 10b
Taxi taxi 5d
Tee tea 10c/14a
Telefon telephone 18c
Telefonbuch telephone directory 18c
telefonieren to phone 18c
Telefonnummer telephone number 18c
Telefonzelle telephone box 18c
Telegramm telegram 18b
Teller plate 10b
Temperatur temperature 17a
Tennis tennis 16c
teuer expensive 6c/9d
Theater theatre 15c
Theke bar, counter 11a
Tief low-pressure area 17c
Tiefgarage underground garage 3d
Tisch table 11a
Toastbrot toast 10c
Toilette toilet 6d
Tomaten tomatoes 13a
Tomatensuppe tomato soup 12a
Tor archway, gate 15bTorte layer cake 13c
Tourist tourist 15a
Treppe stairs 6b
trinken to drink 11b
Trinkgeld tip 11d
trocken dry 17b
Tube tube 19d
Turnschuhe tennis shoes, trainers 19b

U-Bahn underground train 5d
U-Bahn-Station underground station 5d

German-English Vocabulary

Überfahrt crossing 5c
Übernachtung mit Frühstück bed and breakfast 10a
Überlandbus long-distance bus 5d
Uhr clock, watch 8a
Umleitung diversion 3b
umsteigen to change trains 5e
Unfall accident 20a
Untergrundbahn underground train 5d
unterschreiben to sign 2b
Unterschrift signature 2b

Veranstaltung event, function 15c
Verkäuferin shop assistant 9c
verletzt hurt 20d
Verletzte casualty, injured person 20a
verloren lost 20b
Versicherung insurance 20a
Versicherungskarte insurance card 20a
verstehen to understand 2c
verzollen to pay duty on 2a
viel a lot 7b
Vollpension room with 3 meals included 10a
Vormittag morning 8b
Vorname first name 2b
Vorsicht careful 20g
Vorstellung performance 15c
Vorwahl area code 18c

Wagen coach (railway) 5a
Währung currency 9b
Wald wood, forest 16b
Waliser, Waliserin Welsh man, woman 2c
Wanderung hike 16c
wann when 8a
warm warm 17b
warten to wait, hold the line 18c
waschen to wash, shampoo 19e
Wechselkurs exchange rate 9b
Wechselstube currency exchange office 9b
Weg path, way 3b
Wein wine 14b
Weinbrand brandy 14b
Weinkarte wine-list 11b
Weintrauben grapes 13b
Weinstube wine bar 11a
weiß white 19c
weit far 4d
wenig a little 7b
Werkstatt car repair garage 20a
Wertgegenstände valuables 20b
Westen west 4d
Wetter weather 17a
Wetterbericht weather forecast 17a
Wetterlage weather situation 17a
wieviel how much 3c
Wild game 12b
Wind wind 17c
Woche week 8c
Wochenende weekend 8c
wohnen to live 4c
Wohnwagen caravan 3a
wolkig cloudy 17c
Wurst sausage 10c/d
Würstchen pork sausages 10d

zahlen to pay 11d
Zahnarzt dentist 20f
Zahnbürste toothbrush 19d
Zahnpasta toothpaste 19d
Zebrastreifen zebra crossing 4c
Zeit time 20a
Zeitung newspaper 2c
Zentimeter centimetre 7b
Zeuge witness 20a
ziehen to pull 15d
Zigarette cigarette 14c
Zigarre cigar 14c
Zimmer room 6b
Zitrone lemon 13b
Zoll customs 2a
Zucker sugar 11c
zusammen together 11d
Zuschlag surcharge 5e
Zwiebeln onions 13a

English-German Vocabulary

a ein 1e
accident Unfall 20a
address Adresse 2b/18b
admission ticket Eintrittskarte 15c
afternoon Nachmittag 8b
airmail Luftpost 18b
air ticket Flugschein 5b
airport Flughafen 5b
a lot viel, eine Menge 7b
ambulance Krankenwagen 20f
anorak Anorak 19a
apple Apfel 13b
apple juice Apfelsaft 11b
archway Tor 15b
area code Vorwahl 18c
arrival Ankunft 5e
arrive (to) ankommen 8b
ash tray Aschenbecher 14c
asparagus Spargel 13a
Austria Österreich 2c
Australia Australien 2c
Australian Australier, Australierin 2c
avenue Allee 4c

bad schlecht 17c
bag Tasche 2a
balcony Rang 15c
banana Banane 13b
bank Bank 9b
banknote der Schein 9a
bar Theke 11a
barber Friseur 19e
bath Bad 6b
bathe (to) baden 16c
bathing-cap Badekappe 19a
battery Batterie 16d
beach Strand 16b
beans Bohnen 13a
bed Bett 6b
beef Rindfleisch 12b
beer Bier 14b
beverages Getränke 14a
bicycle Fahrrad 3a
big groß 19a
bill Rechnung 6c
biscuit Keks 13c

black schwarz 19c
blouse Bluse 19a
blow-dry (to) föhnen 19e
blue blau 19c
boarding card Bordkarte 5b
boat Boot 16c
boat hire Bootsverleih 16c
boiled gekocht 12b
bon appétit Guten Appetit 11b
book (to) buchen 5b/15a
boot (of car) Kofferraum 2a
boots Stiefel 19b
bottle Flasche 10b
bottle-opener Flaschenöffner 14b
boy Junge 1d
brandy Weinbrand 14b
bread Brot 10c
breakdown Panne 20a
breakfast Frühstück 10a
bridge Brücke 4c
bright heiter 17b
British britisch 2c
brochure Prospekt 15a
broiled chicken Brathähnchen 12c
brown braun 19c
bus Autobus 5d
bus stop Bushaltestelle 5d
butter Butter 10c
buttermilk Buttermilch 14a
button mushrooms Champignons 13a
buy (to) kaufen 9c

cabbage Kohl, Kraut 13a
cabin Kabine 5c
café Café 11a
cake Kuchen 13c
call (to) rufen 20c
camera Fotoapparat, Kamera 16d
campsite Campingplatz 6a
Canadian Kanadisch, Kanadier(in) 2c
car Auto, PKW, Personenkraftwagen 3a, Wagen 5a
car hire Autovermietung 3a
car park Parkplatz 3d
car repair garage Werkstatt 20a
caravan Wohnwagen 3a

English-German Vocabulary

careful Vorsicht 20g
carp Karpfen 12d
carrots Möhren, Mohrrüben 13a
cashier Kasse 9d
cash register Kasse 9d
cash register receipt Kassenbon 9d
castle Burg 15b
casualty Verletzte 20a
cathedral Dom 15b
cauliflower Blumenkohl 13a
caution Achtung 20g
centimetre Zentimeter 7b
champagne Champagner 14b
change Kleingeld 9a, (to) eintauschen 9b
change trains (to) umsteigen 5e
cheap billig 9d
check (to) prüfen 3c
cheque Scheck 9d
cheers Prost 14b
cheese Käse 10c
chemist Apotheke 20e
cherry Kirsche 13b
chicken Hähnchen 12c
chicken soup Hühnersuppe 12a
chips Pommes frites 10d
chocolate Schokolade 13c
chocolate sweet Praline 13c
chop Kotelett 12b
church Kirche 15b
cigar Zigarre 14c
cigarette Zigarette 14c
cinema Kino 15c
city Stadt, Großstadt 4b
city centre Innenstadt 4b
city sightseeing tour Stadtrundfahrt 15a
clear heiter 17b
clearing up Aufheiterung 17b
cloakroom Garderobe 15d
clock Uhr 8a
closed geschlossen 15d
clothing Kleidung 19a
clouds Bewölkung 17c
cloudy wolkig 17c
coach (railway) Wagen 5a
coat Mantel 19a
cocoa Schokolade 14a

cod Kabeljau 12d
coffee Kaffee 10c/14a
coffeepot Kaffeekanne 10b
cold kalt 14a/17d
colour Farbe 19c
comb Kamm 19e
concert-hall Konzerthalle 15c
consulate Konsulat 2c
convent Kloster 15b
cool kuhl 17d
cork screw Korkenzieher 14b
cost (to) kosten 9d
couchette Liegewagen 5a
counter Theke 11a
course Gang 11b
cover (charge) Gedeck 11b
credit card Kreditkarte 9b
crossing Überfahrt 5c
cucumbers Gurken 13a
cup Tasse 10b
currency Währung 9b
currency exchange office
  Wechselstube 9b
customer Kunde 9c
customs Zoll 2a
cutlet Schnitzel 12b

danger Gefahr 20g
date Datum 20a
day Tag 8b
deck Deck 5c
declare (to) anmelden 2a
dentist Zahnarzt 20f
department store Kaufhaus 9c
departure Abfahrt 5e
dessert Nachtisch 11b
diesel Diesel 3c
dinner Abendessen 10a
direction Richtung 4d
diversion Umleitung 3b
docking area Anlegestelle 5c
doctor Arzt 20f
double room Doppelzimmer 6b
dress Kleid 19a
drink (to) trinken 11b
drinks Getränke 14a
drive (to) mit dem Auto fahren 3a

driver Autofahrer 3a
driving licence Führerschein 2b
dry trocken 17b
duck Ente 12c

east Osten 4d
eat (to) essen 10a
egg Ei 10c/12c
electric razor Rasierapparat 19d
embankment Damm 4c
embassy Botschaft 2c
emergency service Notdienst 20f
Englishman Engländer 2c
English woman Engländerin 2c
English englisch 2c
entrance Eingang 15d
evening Abend 8b
event Veranstaltung 15c
every day jeden Tag 8b
exchange rate Wechselkurs 9b
excursion Ausflug 16a
excuse me Entschuldigen Sie 1c
exhibition Ausstellung 15b
exit Ausgang 5b/15d; Ausfahrt 3b
expensive teuer 6c/9d
express train D-Zug 5a; Intercity-Zug 5a; Eilzug 5a

far weit 4d
fare Fahrpreis 5e
Federal Republic of Germany Bundesrepublik Deutschland 2c
ferry Fähre 5c
fever Fieber 20d
fill up (to) tanken 3c
fine Geldstrafe 20c
first aid Erste Hilfe 20f
first name Vorname 2b
fish Fisch 12d
fish fillet Fischfilet 12d
fitting room Anprobe 19a
flash Blitz 16d
flight Flug 5b
floor Stockwerk 6b
fog Nebel 17c
foreigner Ausländer(in) 2c

forest Wald 16b
fork Gabel 10b
fortress Burg 15b
frankfurter (sausage) Bockwurst 10b
fresh frisch 17c
Friday Freitag 8c
fruit Obst, Früchte 13b
function Veranstaltung 15c

gallery Galerie 15b
garage Garage 3d
game (on menu) Wild 12b
gate Ausgang 5b; Tor 15b
gentleman Herr 1d
gentlemen Herren 6d
German deutsch, Deutsche(r) 2c
German Democratic Republic Deutsche Demokratische Republik 2c
German federal railways Deutsche Bundesbahn 5a
Germany Deutschland 2c
girl Mädchen 1d
glass Glas 10b
glasses Brille 19d
go (to) gehen 5b
good afternoon Guten Tag 1b
goodbye Auf Wiedersehen 1b
good evening Guten Abend 1b
good morning Guten Morgen 1b
good night Gute Nacht 1b
good weather schönes Wetter 17c
goulash Gulasch 12b
goulash soup Gulaschsuppe 12a
grain spirit Korn 14b
gram Gramm 7b
grapes Weintrauben 13b
gravel Rollsplitt 3b
gravy Sauce 12b
green grün 19c
grey grau 19c
groceries Lebensmittel 9
ground floor Erdgeschoß 6b
guest Gast 11a
guest house Pension 6a
guidebook Reiseführer 15a

guided tour Führung 15d
gusty böig 17c

hair Haare 19e
hairdresser Friseur 19e
ham Schinken 12b
handbag Handtasche 1e/f
handkerchief Taschentuch 19d
harbour Hafen 5d
hat Hut 19a
headache Kopfschmerzen 20d
heart attack Herzanfall 20d
hello Guten Tag 1b; Hallo 18c
help helfen 9c; Hilfe 20g
herring Hering 12d
high-pressure area Hoch 17b
hike Wanderung 16c
hire (to) leihen 16c
hospital Krankenhaus 20f
hot heiß 17b
hot chocolate Schokolade 14a
hotel Hotel 6a
hotel safe Hotelsafe 20b
hour Stunde 8A
how much Wieviel 3c
hurt verletzt 20d
husband Mann 1f

I ich 1f
ice Eis, Glatteis 17d
ice cream Eis 13c
identity card Ausweis 2b
indoor swimming pool Hallenbad 16c
information Auskunft 5e
information (desk) Information 5e
injured person Verletzte 20
injury Personenschaden 20a
insurance Versicherung 20a
insurance card Versicherungskarte 20a
island Insel 16b

Jacket Jacke 19a
jam Konfitüre 10c
juice Saft 14a

ketchup Ketchup 10d
key Schlüssel 6b
kilogram kilo 7b
kilometre Kilometer 7b
knife Messer 10b

ladies Damen 6d
lady Dame 1d
lake See 16b
lawyer Rechtsanwalt 20c
layer cake Torte 13c
leave (to) abreisen, abfahren 8b
lemon Zitrone 13b
left (nach) links 4d
letter Brief 18b
letter-box Briefkasten 18a
lift Fahrstuhl 6b
lighter Feuerzeug 14c
line Linie 5d
liter Liter 7b
little wenig 7b
live (to) wohnen 4c
liver Leber 12b
local call Ortsgespräch 18c
local commuter train Nahverkehrszug 5a
locker Schließfach 5e
long-distance bus Reisebus 5d
long-distance call Ferngespräch 18c
lorry LKW, Lastkraftwagen 3a
lost verloren 20b
low-pressure area Tief 17c
luggage Gepäck 2a
lunch Mittagessen 10a

main floor Erdgeschoß 6b
main station Hauptbahnhof 5a
main street Hauptstraße 4c
major road Bundesstraße 3b
map Landkarte 4a
mark Mark 9a
market Markt 9c
marzipan Marzipan 13c
match Streichholz 14c
material damage Sachschaden 20a
meat Fleisch 12b

English-German Vocabulary

meatball Frikadelſe 12b
mechanic Automechaniker 20a
menu Speisekarte 11b
menu of the day Tagesmenü 11b
metre Meter 7b
midday Mittag 8b
midnight Mitternacht 8b
milk Milch 14a
mineral water Mineralwasser 14a
minster Münster 15b
minute Minute 8a
moment Augenblick 8a
monastery Kloster 15b
Monday Montag 8c
money Geld 9a
month Monat 8c
more mehr 7b
morning Morgen, Vormittag 8b
motorcycle Motorrad 3A
motorway Autobahn 3b
motorway intersection
  Autobahnkreuz 3b
motorway junction
  Autobahndreieck 3b
mountain Berg 16b
mountain range Gebirge 16b
mountains Gebirge 16b
Mr Herr 1d
Mrs Frau 1d
museum Museum 15b
mushrooms Pilze 13a
mustard Senf 10d
my mein(e) 1f

name Name 2b
narrow street Gasse 4c
nationality Staatsangehörigkeit 2c
newspaper Zeitung 2c
next week nächste Woche 8c
night Nacht 8b
no nein 1a
noodlesoup Nudelsuppe 12a
north Norden 4d
Northern Germany
  Norddeutschland 4a

occupied besetzt 6d
ocean See 16b
ocean perch Rotbarsch 12d
oil Öl 3c
oil change Ölwechsel 3c
omelette Omelett 12c
one-way street Einbahnstraße 4c
onions Zwiebeln 13A
open aufmachen 2a; geöffnet 15d
opening times Öffnungszeiten 15d
opera Oper 15c
operator (telephone) Auskunft 18c
orange Apfelsine 13b
orange-juice Orangensaft 10c
orchestra seats Parkett 15c
order (to) bestellen 11b
outdoor swimming pool Freibad 16c
overcast bedeckt 17c
oxtail soup Ochsenschwanzsuppe 12a

packet of cigarettes Schachtel
  Zigaretten 14c
pair Paar 19b
park (to) parken 3d, Park 16b
parking fee Parkgebuhr 3d
parking garage Parkhaus 3d
parking metre Parkuhr 3d
parking spot Parkplatz 3d
passport Reisepaß 2b
passport control Paßkontrolle 2b
path Weg 3b
pay (to) bezahlen 3d/9d, zahlen 11d
pay by cheque (to) mit Scheck bezahlen 9d
pay duty on (to) verzollen 2a
pay in cash (to) bar bezahlen 9d
peach Pfirsich 13b
pear Birne 13b
peas Erbsen 13a
pedestrian Fußgänger 4c
pedestrian shopping precinct
  Fußgängerzone 4c
pepper Pfeffer 11c
performance Vorstellung 15c
petrol Benzin 3c
petrol station Tankstelle 3c
pheasant Fasan 12c

English-German Vocabulary

phone (to) telefonieren 18c
photo Foto 16d
piece Stück 19d
pill Tablette 20e
pils Pils 14b
pipe Pfeife 14c
place Ort 20a
plaice Scholle 12d
plaster Pflaster 20e
plate Teller 10b
platform Gleis 5a
please bitte 1c
police Polizei 20c
policeman Polizist 20c
pork Schweinefleisch 12b
pork sausages Würstchen 10d
port Hafen 5c
postcard Postkarte 18b
postcode Postleitzahl 18b
post office Post 18a
pot Kännchen 14a
potatoes Kartoffeln 13a
potato salad Kartoffelsalat 10d
poultry Geflügel 12c
pound Pfund 7b
precipitation Niederschlag 17c
price Preis 6c/9d
print Foto 16d
pull (to) ziehen 15d
pullover Pullover 19a
purse Portemonnaie 20b
push (to) drücken 15d

quick bite Imbiß 10d

railway Eisenbahn 5a
railway station Bahnhof 5a
rain Regen 17c; **(to)** regnen 17c
raspberries Himbeeren 13b
razor-blades Rasierklingen 19d
receipt Quittung 9d
reception (desk) Rezeption 6b
red rot 19c
rent, hire leihen 16c
report (to) melden 20a
reserved reserviert 11a

restaurant Restaurant 11a
rest stop Raststätte 3b
return ticket Rückfahrkarte 5e
rice Reis 13a
right (nach) rechts 4d
river Fluß 16b
road map Straßenkarte 4a
roll Brötchen 10c
room Zimmer 6b
row Reihe 5b/15c

sail (to) segeln 16c
sale item Sonderangebot 9c
salt Salz 11c
sanitary towel Damenbinde 19d
Saturday Samstag 8c
sauce Sauce 12b
sausage Wurst 10c/d
savings and loan association Sparkasse 9b
scarf Schal 19a
Scotsman, woman Schotte, Schottin 2c
scrambled eggs Rührei 12c
sea See 16b
seat Sitz 5b/15c; Platz 11a
seat reservation Platzreservierung 5e
secondary road Landstraße 3b
security check Sicherheitskontrolle 5b
self-service Selbstbedienung 11a
sender Absender 18b
service (included) Trinkgeld (inbegriffen) 11d
shampoo Shampoo 19d
shave Rasur 19e
shine (to) scheinen 17b
ship Schiff 5c
shirt Oberhemd 19a
shoes Schuhe 19b
shop Geschäft 9c
shop-assistant Verkäuferin 9c
shopping centre Einkaufszentrum 9c
shower Dusche 6b; Schauer 17c
shrimp Krabbe 12d
sick krank 20d
sights Sehenswürdigkeiten 15b

English-German Vocabulary

sightseeing trip Rundfahrt 16a
sign (to) unterschreiben 2b
signature Unterschrift 2b
single room Einzelzimmer 6b
size Größe 19a
ski (to) Ski laufen 16c
skirt Rock 19a
sleep (to) schlafen 20d
sleeping car Schlafwagen 5a
sleeping pill Schlaftablette 20e
slice Scheibe 10c
slide Dia 16d
slowly langsam 4
small motorcycle Moped 3a
smoke (to) rauchen 14c
snack Imbiß 10d
snack bar Imbißstube 10d
snow Schnee, **(to)** schneien 17d
soap Seife 19d
soccer Fußball 16c
socks Socken 19b
sole Seezunge 12d
sorry: I'm sorry Es tut mit leid 1c
soup Suppe 12a
soup of the day Tagessuppe 12a
south Süden 4d
sparkling wine Sekt 14b
spoon Löffel 10b
square Platz 4c
stairs Treppe 6b
stamp Briefmarke 18b
steak Steak 12b
stockings Strümpfe 19b
stolen gestohlen 20b
stomachache Magenschmerzen 20d
store Geschäft 9c
storm Sturm 17c
straight ahead geradeaus 4d
strawberry Erdbeere 13b
street Straße 4c
stroll Spaziergang 16c
strong stark 17c
suburban railway Schnellbahn 5d
sugar Zucker 11c
suitcase Koffer 2a
sun Sonne 17b
Sunday Sonntag 8c
sunglasses Sonnenbrille 19d

sunny sonnig 17b
sunshine Sonnenschein 17b
supermarket Supermarkt 19c
supper Abendbrot, Abendessen 10a
surcharge Zuschlag 5e
surfboard Surfbrett 16c
sweater Pullover 19a
sweets Konfekt 13c
swim (to) baden, schwimmen 16c
swimming trunks Badehose 19a
swimming costume Badeanzug 19a
Switzerland Schweiz 2c

table Tisch 11a
take (to) nehmen 19a
taken besetzt 11a
tampon Tampon 19d
taxi Taxi 5d
tea Tee 10c/14a
telegram Telegramm 18b
telephone Telefon 18c
telephone box Telefonzelle 18c
telephone directory Telefonbuch 18c
telephone number Telefonnummer 18c
temperature Temperatur 17a
tennis Tennis 16c
tennis shoes Turnschuhe 19b
thank you danke 1c
the der, die, das 1e
theatre Theater 15c
through coach Kurswagen 5a
thunderstorm Gewitter 17c
Thursday Donnerstag 8c
ticket Fahrkarte 5e
tie Krawatte 19a
tight klein 19a
tights Strumpfhose 19b
time Zeit 20a
timetable Fahrplan 5e
tip Trinkgeld 11d
toast Toastbrot 10c
tobacco Tabak 14c
today heute 8b
together zusammen 11d
toilet Toilette 6d
tomatoes Tomaten 13a

English-German Vocabulary

tomato soup Tomatensuppe 12a
tomorrow Morgen 8b
toothbrush Zahnbürste 19d
toothpaste Zahnpasta 19d
tour guide Reiseleiter 15a
tourist Tourist 15a
towel Handtuch 19d
town Kleinstadt 4b
town hall Rathaus 4b
town map Stadtplan 4a
track Gleis 5a
trade fair Messe 15b
traffic jam Stau 3b
traffic light(s) Ampel 4c
travel agency Reisebüro 15a
traveller's cheque Reisescheck 9b
travel guide Reiseführer 15a
trip Reise 15a; Ausflug 16a
trousers Hose 19a
trout Forelle 12d
tube Tube 19d
Tuesday Dienstag 8c
turn (to) abbiegen 4d
tyre Reifen 3c

umbrella Regenschirm 17c
underground garage Tiefgarage 3d
underground U-Bahn,
  Untergrundbahn 5d
understand verstehen 2c
unleaded bleifrei 3c

VAT Mehrwerksteuer 9d
vacant frei 6d
valley Tal 16b
valuables Wertgegenstände 20b
veal Kalbfleisch 12b
vegetables Gemüse 13a
village Dorf 4b
vinegar Essig 11c

wait warten 18c
waiter Kellner, Ober 11d
waitress Fräulein 11d
walk Spaziergang 16c
wallet Brieftasche 20b
warm warm 17b
wash (to) waschen 19e
watch Uhr 8a
watch out Achtung 20g
way Weg 3b
weather Wetter 17a
weather forecast Wetterbericht 17a
weather situation Wetterlage 17a
Wednesday Mittwoch 8c
week Woche 8c
weekend Wochenende 8c
Welshman, woman Waliser, Walisin
  2c
west Westen 4d
when wann 8a
whipped cream Schlagsahne 13c
white weiß 19c
wife Frau 1f
wind Wind 17c
wine Wein 14b
wine tavern Weinstube 11a
witness Zeuge 20a
woman Frau 1d
wood Wald 16b

year Jahr 8c
yellow gelb 19c
yes ja 1a
yesterday gestern 8b
you du, Sie 1f
young lady Fräulein 1d
your dein(e), Ihr(e) 1f
youth hostel Jugendherberge 6a

zebra crossing Zebrastreifen 4c

British Library Cataloguing in Publication Data

Lübke Diethard
Quick and easy German—(Teach yourself books)
1. German Language—Spoken German
2. German Language—Text-books for foreign
speakers—English
I. Title
438.3'421   PF3121

ISBN 0 340 38765 3

Teach Yourself edition first published 1986
Reissued 1993
Impression number   18 17 16 15 14
Year   1999 1998 1997 1996 1995

Adapted from the original Langenscheidt edition by Sarah Boas.
Langenscheidt edition by Diethard Lübke, copyright © 1984 by
Langenscheidt KG, Berlin and Munich.
Illustrations by Herbert Horn.

Typeset by Macmillan India Ltd, Bangalore 25.
Printed and bound in Great Britain for Hodder & Stoughton
Educational, a division of Hodder Headline Plc, 338 Euston Road,
London NW1 3BH by Cox & Wyman Ltd, Reading, Berkshire.